KITTLER AND THE MEDIA

Theory and Media

KITTLER AND THE MEDIA

GEOFFREY WINTHROP-YOUNG

polity

First published in 2011 by Polity Press

Polity Press
65 Bridge Street
Cambridge CB2 1UR, UK

Polity Press
350 Main Street
Malden, MA 02148, USA

ISBN-13: 978-0-7456-4405-9
ISBN-13: 978-0-7456-4406-6(pb)

A catalogue record for this book is available from the British Library.

Typeset in 10.75 on 14 pt Janson Text
by Servis Filmsetting Ltd, Stockport, Cheshire
Printed and bound in Great Britain by the MPG Books Group

CONTENTS

ACKNOWLEDGMENTS

The following overview is the first book-length introduction to Kittler's work in English. In preparing the text I have drawn on material published elsewhere (especially Winthrop-Young 2002; 2005; 2006b; Winthrop-Young and Wutz 1999; and Winthrop-Young and Gane 2006) and profited from helpful input by John Armitage, Michael Berger, Claudia Breger, Frank Hartmann, Till Heilmann, Philipp von Hilgers, Sybille Krämer, Geert Lovink, Larson Powell, Cornelia Vismann, Hartmut Winkler, and Michael Wutz. I am especially indebted to John Durham Peters, who always comes up with a better way of putting things.

INTRODUCTION

Fame, in the words of the poet Rainer Maria Rilke, is no more than the sum of all the misunderstandings that cling to a name. The recent fame of Friedrich Kittler is no exception. To his English-speaking audience he is known either as Germany's leading media theorist or as one of the most influential German proponents of poststructuralism. Sometimes the tags are stitched together and Kittler emerges as the leading German poststructuralist media theorist. An impressive and slightly intimidating label, no doubt, but how accurate is it?

To begin with, Kittler did not start out as a *media* theorist. His early work from the 1970s dealt with literary texts rather than with media technologies. The very words "medium" and "media" hardly occurred, and he never referred to himself as a media theorist. To make matters worse, his most recent work on the evolution of alpha-numerical sign systems appears to place him outside of conventional media studies. But if the young Kittler was not yet a media theorist and the older Kittler is no longer one (at least, not in the usual sense of the term), how useful is the designation? Concerning the slippery label *poststructuralism*, while Kittler did employ it at the outset of his career (one of his early edited volumes was subtitled "Programs of Poststructuralism"), the term soon disappears. Even worse, it is ridiculed by Kittler, whose work in fact raises doubt whether it should have been used at all. And what about the most troubling tag, *German*? It is a bit of an insult. The overwhelming presence of the Anglo-American academic industry in media and communication studies is such that many anglophone practitioners no longer consider it necessary to situate their work by using national adjectives, yet contributions that originate elsewhere need to be labeled "French," "German," or "Japanese." These appellations do not refer to anything specific to France, Germany, or Japan, but merely serve to indicate that the work in question is *not* English. Nonetheless, the label *German* can and should be applied to Kittler. It does not, however, stand for any essential national characteristic (as if such natural collective attributes existed) but for a discursive context that arose in Germany even before the state bearing that name came into existence. Kittler's theory is not German because he was born in Germany or writes in German, or because he frequently draws on canonized German names such as Hegel, Nietzsche, or Heidegger. (By the same token, he could be labeled French in light of his indebtedness to Michel Foucault and Jacques Lacan, American because of his high regard for Claude Shannon and Thomas Pynchon, or even British given his veneration of Alan Turing and Pink Floyd.) He has produced a German theory because the deeper layers of his work, the bias of his arguments and the recurrence of a certain set of references and associations, not to mention the way in which he expresses them, have to be understood against the background of debates about technology, humanism, and individual as well as collective identity formation that over the course of the last two centuries emerged in the German-speaking countries.

To simplify matters, this introduction will treat Kittler's work as a sequence made up of three stages. The first stage, which lasted from the mid-1970s to the early 1980s, focused on texts, more precisely, on the *discourse analysis* or "archeology" of primarily literary texts. The second stage, which started in the early 1980s and lasted for roughly two decades, concentrated on *media technologies*, first on the new, primarily analog media of the late nineteenth century (phonography, cinematography, the typewriter-induced mechanization of writing) and then on digital technology. While Kittler himself may not be too happy about it, this second, media-based stage is generally regarded to be his most important contribution; it is certainly the most widely translated portion of his work. The third stage, at the center of which is a large-scale, ontologically oriented genealogy of mathematical and musical notation systems, engages *cultural techniques* (*Kulturtechniken*), a complex term greatly in vogue in current German theory that combines an attention to media technologies with a focus on elementary physical and mental skills, including, most prominently, reading, writing, and computing. With this tripartite division in mind, we shall start with a biographical overview that will introduce readers to some of the important connections between Kittler's work and the changing historical, political, and intellectual German environments (chapter 1). Chapters 2, 3, and 4 will deal with his analyses of texts, media technologies, and Greek alphanumerical cultural techniques, respectively. Each chapter begins with an opening teaser, that is, with an analysis by Kittler of a short "text" that contains in a nutshell the salient points of that particular stage. These texts have been chosen because each of them constitutes, to introduce the first item of vintage Kittlerese, a "discourse on discourse channel conditions." They are messages about their own medium, they discuss and perform their own medial conditions, and are thus highly revealing instances of the media conditions of their day.

Of course, this neat subdivision of Kittler's career into separate stages should not be taken too seriously. It is a heuristic device employed for didactic purposes. Intellectual growth processes do not resemble geological strata; theories rarely evolve in discontinuous leaps and bounds. Kittler did not simply stop writing about literary texts in the early 1980s; neither has he altogether abandoned media and media theory now. Focusing on the noticeable continuities, rather than on the ruptures, we can just as well describe Kittler's work as a widening spiral in which similar questions recur, but each time on a more expansive level. The (very ambitious) spatio-temporal expansion is obvious: the "literature stage" focused almost exclusively on German literature from the so-called age of Goethe (1770–1830); the "media stage" expanded the scope to incorporate almost 200 years of media-technological development in Europe and North America; and the recent "cultural techniques" stage aims at nothing less than the whole of occidental history from ancient Greece to the Gutenberg galaxy and beyond into the Turing age. And while each level calls for different concepts and categories, key concerns remain the same – heteronomy, codes, programming, conflict, and the very characteristic Kittlerian tendency to move between intoxication and investigation, or rapture and rule analysis. It is important that students with an interest in media theory keep this in mind when they wade through chapter 2, wondering what on earth all the analyses of love and language, mothers and ministries, family codes and writing lessons have to do with media. Much of what Kittler will have to say later on about media is already present when he performs his particular discourse analysis of literary texts; and it will remain in place when he takes aim at the singular cultural accomplishments of ancient Greece.

But an important word of caution before we start. Kittler, arguably one of the most complex and baffling contemporary German theorists, is certainly one of the most controversial. He is difficult to read, even more difficult to translate, and almost impossible to discuss without getting mired in the standard objections that accuse him of obscurantism, anti-humanism, techno-determinism, and a faintly Teutonic military fetish. To be sure, he is anything but an innocent target. Kittler generously indulges in provocations and exaggerations, displaying all the gleeful rambunctiousness of a bull that specializes in the destruction of politically correct china shops. In the concluding chapter 5 we will therefore spend a lot of time discussing Kittler's controversial aspects, especially the troublesome three *W*s: war, women, and writing style. As we shall see, some of the usual objections raised against him are off-target, but nonetheless readers should be cautioned right from the start against certain basic expectations that Kittler most certainly will *not* meet.

Many students of media and communication approach the field with a certain idealism. After all, why study media, why meticulously dissect the ways in which cultures process data, why wrestle with increasingly complex media-theoretical proposals, not to mention the politically fraught issues of media access and ownership, if not with some view toward improving matters? No doubt many readers expect that a focused engagement with a high-profile media theorist will result in some insight into media abuse and provide clues as to how we can curb media manipulation, clear the conduits of communication, fully realize the potential of our technologies, or empower the disenfranchised. The idea that someone would spend decades trying to understand media while neglecting, denying, at times even ridiculing such aspirations – that idea is difficult to grasp. Kittler is that someone. His work will strike many as profoundly asocial or even ahuman, especially when approached in a more idealistic spirit. In his texts you will rarely encounter the words *Gesellschaft* (society) or *Aufklärung* (enlightenment) without hearing a sneer. *Mensch* – "human" or "man" – is almost always (dis)qualified as *der sogenannte Mensch* ("so-called man"), Kittler prefers the unassuming and in an academic context slightly dismissive *Leute* ("people" or "folks"). This is not because he disapproves of emancipatory socio-political agendas, but because these approaches are in his eyes based on naive conceptualizations of media that do not take into account the degree to which, to quote his most (in)famous opening line, "[m]edia determine our situation" (Kittler 1999: 1) – especially when we believe that we can determine *them* while pursuing our worthy social goals.

The German poet Gottfried Benn, who occupies a prominent seat in Kittler's personal pantheon, once remarked that "the opposite of art is not nature but well meant (*gut gemeint*)" (Benn II, 1984: 156). This can be read as a radicalization of T. S. Eliot's famous axiom that "[t]he more perfect the artist, the more completely separate in him will be the man who suffers and the mind which creates; the more perfectly will the mind digest and transmute the passions which are its material" (Eliot 2005: 154). Art – real art that deserves its name – is cold. Or, as nineteenth-century French thinkers liked to point out, art (pronounced in French with a nasal *a* and no *t*) is the sound an eagle makes when it swoops down on its prey. A good poem is made of words, not of feelings; it is clinical, technical, distant, removed, almost arctic in its isolation and therefore exceedingly rare, as opposed to the well-intentioned verbiage emanating from salons, seminars, or barricades designed to soothe, instruct, or mobilize impressionable readers. A similar axiom could be applied to Kittler's self-understanding as a theorist: *the opposite of theory is not practice but well meant.* Good theory does little to improve the human lot; it does not make the world a better place; it merely serves to make it a bit more inhospitable for bad – that is, naive, sentimental, uninformed, serenely clueless, and hopelessly deluded – theorizing. To use the biased and often unapologetically macho thermal metaphors that Kittler and those writing in his wake are so fond of, this particular type of media theory sees itself as a necessary cold-water current injected into notoriously warm waters. We will have to investigate what this current consists of, where it originates, and how it enriches the larger streams it enters.

1

BACKGROUND – BIOGRAPHY AND BEYOND

1. AFTER STALINGRAD

The philosopher Martin Heidegger (who will haunt this introduction just as he has haunted Kittler's career) once summarized the life of Aristotle in a memorably economic way: "He was born, worked, and died." In other (and more) words: Aristotle's importance resides in what he thought; whatever else he may have done on the side – living, getting involved in Athenian politics, attempting to turn the young Alexander the Great into a responsible adult – is not worth talking about. Though still alive, Kittler seems ideally suited for Heidegger's pithy summary.

Friedrich Adolf Kittler was born on June 12, 1943, in Rochlitz, a small town in Saxony close to Germany's eastern border. In 1958 his family relocated to Lahr, a small town in the Black Forest near Germany's western border. After finishing high school in 1963 he enrolled in German, Romance studies, and philosophy at the nearby Albert-Ludwigs

University in Freiburg. In 1976 he completed a PhD on the Swiss nineteenth-century writer Conrad Ferdinand Mayer, after which he worked as a lecturer at the German department in Freiburg. Following the completion of his *Habilitation* (the second, more extensive dissertation that qualifies candidates to formally teach at a German university) in 1985, he was briefly employed in Basel before becoming Professor of Modern German Literature at the University of Bochum in 1987. In 1993 he was appointed Chair of Media Aesthetics at the prestigious Humboldt University in the newly reunited Berlin. He retired in 2008 but now holds (still at the Humboldt University) an Endowed Guest Professorship in Media Philosophy. In over thirty years of academic labor he has written and edited more than two dozen books and well over twelve dozen papers. To paraphrase Heidegger, he was born, worked, and goes on working. Kittler's career is at first glance a stereotypical academic existence, a life spent between libraries and lecture halls. But peel away the scholarly veneer of this biography and aspects will emerge that are of help when it comes to understanding some of the hidden historical and cultural undercurrents that influence his work.

Rochlitz is located in the vicinity of Dresden, a city some readers may associate with the controversial air raid of February 13–15, 1945. In a recent interview Kittler mentioned that he dimly recalls "the fires over Dresden at night" (Armitage 2006: 26), which is a remarkable feat of memory given that at the time he was a few months shy of his second birthday. Let us treat it as a symbolic reminiscence that sheds first light on one of the most controversial aspects of his work. Kittler is a so-called Stalingrad child; he was born during the Third Reich but after the catastrophic defeat that caused a growing number of Germans to lose faith in the military prowess of the regime. It became obvious to many that the war could no longer be won on Germany's terms;

and given the intransigence of the Nazi regime it would
probably end in total defeat. Yet now something strange
happened. Following Stalingrad, the total mobilization of
Germany turned the war into an inescapable, all-pervasive
presence that more than ever dominated every aspect of life.
Following the German surrender in May 1945, however, the
war was, as it were, robbed of its stature to such an extent
that it appeared not to have taken place – or at least not in
the way many had experienced it. Yet at the same time the
war continued in ways that left an indelible impression on
Kittler's childhood.

Rochlitz was part of the Soviet-occupied zone which in
1949 mutated into the short-lived German Democratic
Republic (GDR), better known as East Germany. Claiming
to have broken with all the authoritarian and fascist tradi-
tions that allegedly were still at large in West Germany, the
GDR presented itself as the true fulfillment of past dreams
of progress and enlightenment. *Real existierender Sozialismus*
("really existing socialism") had finally come to Germany, if
only to one third of its territory. This flattering self-image
of the GDR as the legitimate heir to the better angels of
German history shaped its official view of the war. The defeat
at the hands of the Red Army was celebrated as a liberation
from tyranny achieved by the heroic efforts of the workers
and soldiers of the Soviet Union. No doubt this account
corresponded to the perceptions of those who had suffered
under the Nazi regime and who were now engaged in building a better Germany, but in many other cases it opened a
rift between the officially sanctioned view of the war and
individual experiences. State-imposed history marginalized
private memories – a conspicuous divide that also occurred
in West Germany. While World War I became the war
that could not find its name because its unexpected horrors
outstripped the ability to experience them in a meaningful

way, World War II, whose engineered horrors were better known, seemed to turn into the war that dare not speak its name.

But the partly suppressed war was bound to resurface in all sorts of places, including the Kittler household. In a book-length interview Kittler recounts how his elder half-brother, a former wireless operator, used his technical expertise to assemble illegal radios by using parts scavenged from abandoned military aircraft in order to impress the local girls (Kittler and Banz 1996: 47). At the same time, his father, a teacher who had lost most of his students to the war, took to lecturing his children instead, with the result that by age seven Kittler was able to recite long passages from Goethe's *Faust* off by heart. Thus, at a very early stage, much of what later came to dominate Kittler's work was already in place, from the pre-established discursive order that ensnares children in the humanist universe to the emergence of civilian recording and broadcasting technology as an "abuse of army equipment" (Kittler 1999: 97). The juxtaposition of Goethe and the radio, classicism and technology, high literature and modern media, already contains the contrast between the "Discourse Network 1800" and the "Discourse Network 1900" that Kittler would elaborate three decades later. And we also have the biographical background for Kittler's controversial attempts to relate modern war (and World War II in particular) not to stories of politics and ideology, crime and guilt, or tyranny and liberation, but to the evolution of modern control, communications, and computing technology.

2. HEIDEGGER'S LAIR

Kittler has stated that one of the reasons for the family's move to West Germany was his parents' wish to secure for their children the kind of university education that could not be had in the East. It was this particular background, he adds, that made him "such a keen student" who "was really engaged with the university," unlike many others "who simply went there on the understanding that it was their right to do so, or as a kind of hobby" (Armitage 2006: 17). Kittler, no doubt, was a good student, but this is a somewhat biased assessment of the general student body in the early 1960s, when German universities, intent on overcoming the traditional hierarchy of the German education system, were striving to include larger portions of low-income families that certainly did not view post-secondary education as a "hobby." There is something else at work here: just as his family did not leave the East solely in search of superior institutions of higher learning, the distinction between Kittler the keen and his spoilt peers is covering a more fundamental divide. Like many others, the Kittlers left the GDR because they were politically at odds with the socialist regime; but now, upon entering the university in the early 1960s, Kittler found himself surrounded by an increasing number of fellow students flaunting leftish ideals. This is an important point that is not adequately captured if one simply labels Kittler a conservative. As already noted, Kittler is prone to dismiss individual and collective emancipatory ideals – be it the formation and subsequent sovereignty of the human subject or the ability to engage in meaningful communication for the common pursuit of lofty goals of humanity – as cultural programs that have been inscribed into people and that are so successful because they are mistaken as emanations of a so-called free will. This debunking is to a considerable degree rooted in the divide, as it must have appeared to the young Kittler, between his own childhood experiences of socialism and the abstract socialist rhetoric of his new surroundings.

Kittler spent almost a quarter of a century at the

University of Freiburg. Given his claim that we are "produced by our schools, by our universities and by our lecturers" (Armitage 2006: 24), it is worth taking a look at this lengthy association. Kittler's student years from freshman status to dissertation coincided with the rise and fall of the so-called *Studentenbewegung* or students' movement, the cultural upheaval that in German is encapsulated in shorthand as "1968." The politically inflected label for the generation that came of age in the 1960s is *Achtundsechziger*, the "68ers." Kittler, however, was neither politically active nor particularly interested in expanding his political consciousness. Looking back, the most memorable event of his student days was neither a sit-in nor a demonstration, and not even a consciousness-raising revelation courtesy of Georg Lukács or the Frankfurt School, but a lecture by the modernist composer György Ligeti (Kittler 2006a: 339). While many others (though probably not as many as later claimed) marched in the streets, Kittler sat in his room listening to late Beatles and early Pink Floyd LPs – a preference he attributes to "50% laziness and 50% conservatism" (Kittler and Maresch 1994: 95). To label this the apolitical stance of a right-wing slacker, or the snobby withdrawal from street-level activism, is to apply a fairly narrow interpretation of 1968 that misses out on its hidden undercurrents. For what was Kittler doing in his room apart from listening to *The White Album* and *The Piper at the Gates of Dawn?* He was reading; and among his preferred authors were not only Heidegger and Nietzsche (certainly not the politically correct authors in 1968), but also a phalanx of new French theorists on the verge of crossing the Rhine into Germany: Michel Foucault, Jacques Lacan, and Jacques Derrida. And this is where Freiburg – which in comparison to Frankfurt or Berlin had only been a second-tier center of action in the upheavals of the 1960s – starts to get interesting.

Robert Holub, one of the first scholars to introduce Kittler to an anglophone audience, pointed out that Freiburg and Berlin feature prominently in the German reception of French poststructuralism (Holub 1992: 43). Berlin – to be historically more accurate, the old West Berlin – is an obvious venue: an isolated pressure-cooker metropolis perched on the needlepoint of global politics, a hotbed of 1960s student radicalism with a thriving art scene, swamped by high-school graduates making use of the city's exemption from compulsory military service – how could it not be a receptive entry point for the nomadic, anarchic ideas heading eastward over the Rhine? But Freiburg? That scenic deposit of philistine comfort besieged not by Soviet tanks but the sleepy firs of the Black Forest? Various explanations have been offered to account for its high profile in the German reception of poststructuralism. Some emphasize the city's closeness to France; others invoke the (especially in death) larger-than-life presence of Heidegger. Both explanations are flawed. Geographical proximity has little to do with intellectual contact, especially in densely populated European countries boasting excellent highways and railway systems. Likewise, while many Freiburg visits by the new French luminaries included pilgrimages up the Todtnauberg to gawk at Heidegger's mythical Black Forest cabin, the cloned Heideggerians in the Freiburg philosophy department were no more inclined to engage with the new-fangled Parisian theories than their colleagues elsewhere. To be sure, Freiburg's location allowed the young Kittler to undertake fortnightly excursions to nearby Strasburg in France to attend lectures on Lacan; and it was a factor in securing Lacan's much-anticipated trip to Freiburg in January 1975. The visit, however, was no great success. As he was prone to do, Lacan came, spoke, and left everyone confused. According to Kittler, Lacan "wanted to be influential in

Germany," yet, when he realized how young and lacking in influence Kittler and his associates were, "he was most disappointed" (Armitage 2006: 22). For all his cryptic aloofness, Lacan was a no-nonsense empire builder with an eye for promising beachheads in virgin markets, and Freiburg did not qualify. A few years later Derrida made an appearance and gave a lecture that was translated and edited by Kittler, but while the two over the years enjoyed a cordial relationship, their intellectual differences were so great that they could only be covered by the catch-all label of poststructuralism. The most sought-after theorist was Foucault, whose books the young Kittler awaited as impatiently "as new Rock LPs or the approaching steps [of a lover]" (1985: 141). Eagerly, Kittler kept inviting him; politely, Foucault kept declining. Heidegger or not, Freiburg's allure had its limits.

In fact, Kittler never did meet Foucault, though he did run into him once. In 1976, during the intermission of the last, legendary centenary performance of Richard Wagner's *Ring* cycle, staged by Pierre Boulez and Patrice Chéreau in Bayreuth, he caught sight of a laughing Foucault surrounded by a throng of admirers. But much like Dante in the presence of his beloved Beatrice, Kittler remained frozen and dumbfounded: "I did not approach him" (Kittler 1985: 151). In retrospect, the meeting place is not without a certain ironic symbolism, for in Kittler's eyes the operas of Wagner represent "a monomaniacal anticipation of modern media technologies" (1990: 23; for a detailed analysis, see Kittler 1994). That is to say, the media magician Wagner with his early Sensurround *Gesamtkunstwerk* – what has been described as "Pink Floyd in Bayreuth" (Bolz 1990: 49–65) – is bidding farewell to the world of books and libraries that nurtured and confined the work of Foucault.

A more plausible reason for Freiburg's conspicuous role in the history of German poststructuralism is its *spiritus loci*

– the city's remarkable local political (sub)culture. With its wide array of alternative lifestyle groups, peace activists, radical regionalists, ecological fundamentalists, not to mention the leftovers from the old tradition of Southwest German radical liberalism and a sizeable portion of New Age apostles, Freiburg boasted a highly diverse intellectual milieu that left its mark on local politics as well as on the intellectual endeavors of many students and younger faculty members. While it would be difficult to trace how exactly this countercultural mélange inscribed itself into Kittler's work, there can be no doubt that he profited from an intellectual climate that was comparatively open to the discussion of maverick theories. Freiburg's wayward local radicalism provided fertile grounds for the spread of ideas from across the Rhine which, though located for the most part on the left, frequently defied left-wing orthodoxy. But ultimately it may boil down to simple chance: that at a certain point in time a number of young scholars interested in the new French *pensée sauvage* happened to be located in one and the same provincial town in the Black Forest, which for a brief and shining moment became the makeshift Camelot of German poststructuralism. One thing is certain: those days – Kittler wistfully refers to them as his old "fairy-tale time" (2006a: 339) – are long gone.

3. FRENCH STRUGGLES AT ABBEY ROAD

But, regardless of where the formative German appropriations of French theory took place (it is no coincidence that Kittler transferred to the University of Bochum which had been at the forefront of the German reception of Foucault), it remained a tricky affair. This is crucial to understanding what the young Kittler had to say and why he chose to express it with considerable panache.

But right here we have to pause and sound another note of caution. While there have been initial attempts to chronicle and discuss the US reception of so-called French theory (Cusset 2008; Lotringer and Cohen 2001), no such projects have been undertaken in Germany. The wounds are still fresh; the past is not yet dead enough for impartial autopsy. Inevitably, the next couple of pages (which like the preceding paragraphs are based in part on personal recollections of studying in Freiburg in the 1980s) will not meet with general approval. Those who had or who still have a stake in old theory wars will dismiss a lot of what is to come as a one-sided caricature. But rather than attempting a measured account of what happened in Germany and the United States when a motley crew of French brigands allegedly set out to hijack Western humanism, the following pages will focus on the conspicuous contrasts between the two countries – contrasts which tend to reveal each other's shortcomings. It is precisely the aggressive, uncompromising, polemical German attack on French theory that makes the American reception appear less impressive, self-serving, if not pathetic in many respects; in turn, it is the more detailed, rigorous American engagement with Derrida et al. that serves to highlight the blinkered obsessions shaping the German debate. Future intellectual historians will no doubt map out a common middle ground, but like all such zones of appeasement it will be flat and uninspiring, especially when it comes to discussing the work of a key player who so clearly eschewed all compromise.

Poststructuralism, to put it mildly, did not enjoy a warm welcome in Germany. Its difficult reception was in many ways the opposite of its more spectacular take-off in the United States, where the work of Derrida, Lacan, and Foucault was received at elite institutions (Johns Hopkins, Berkeley, and Cornell, not to mention the "Yale School of

Deconstruction") and then percolated downward and outward. Germany, on the other hand, had little to offer apart from a small, dispersed coterie of for the most part untenured scholars who lacked a spiritual father as well as an intellectual center (Holub 1992: 43). As a result, the German reception tended to start at the margins (students, junior academics, minor publishing houses), and then, gradually, move inward and upward.

In both the United States and Germany the initial fate of the poststructuralist import came to depend in no small degree on what was going on in literature departments. For decades New Criticism had been the dominant force in American literary criticism, but by the early 1960s this had run its course. The deconstructive method championed by Derrida was an uncannily ideal replacement. On the one hand, it was new and – true to the spirit of the sixties – radical in its unabashed critique of the most cherished and unquestioned basics of literary scholarship: the unity of the work, the ability to arrive at a clear message, and the presumed function of literature to transmit so-called timeless values. On the other hand (though practitioners were not too keen to admit this), many of the deconstructive techniques employed to tease out the warring significations in a given text resembled the formalist techniques that New Criticism had employed to probe a text's ambiguities, tensions, and paradoxes. The skills fostered by New Criticism to reverse-engineer a text (let's take it apart to show how it works) remained very much in demand when it came to deconstructing a text (let's take it apart to show that it never worked as intended in the first place). This similarity was enhanced by the fact that deconstruction and New Criticism shared dim views of competing approaches that stressed social or historical circumstances and influences, or that paid sustained attention to what the author tried to say or how the text impacts the reader – what in the parlance of New Criticism was known as the intentional and affective fallacies. In view of what happened in Germany it appears that US-style deconstruction allowed a sizeable number of literary scholars to have their cake and eat it (and hopefully take over the baking shop): it enabled them to continue their business as usual – that is, analyze texts with little regard for social context – but it also gave them the feeling of being engaged in a tremendously radical activity, since the principles of deconstruction could be – and indeed soon were – applied to many extra-literary meaning edifices, including the fundamental narratives of progress and emancipation that academics located further to the left were still clinging to. Bluntly put, a lot of early deconstruction was New Criticism with an attitude. The ivory towers of New Criticism were razed, but a lot of the debris was recycled to erect the ivory barricades of early poststructuralist scholarship.

The situation was different in Germany. The radical niche that poststructuralism managed to occupy in the United States was largely taken over by the strong left-wing currents that swept German literary scholarship in the 1960s. In collective academic memory two conferences that coincidentally both took place in 1966 have come to represent the inter-generational passing of the critical baton. In the United States the Johns Hopkins Conference on the Humanities, which featured performances by Roland Barthes, Jacques Lacan, and Jacques Derrida, is now seen as the foundational event of the American appropriation of French theory (Cusset 2008: 29–32). At about the same time an annual meeting of Germanists in Munich signaled the uprising of the younger, politically more active generation against decades of deeply conservative scholarship whose predilection for apolitical, close textual reading resembled New Criticism. But the German rupture with established critical tradition came with a lot more historical baggage. Many of the leading Germanists of the 1950s and early 1960s had been trained in the Third Reich, some of them had already achieved a certain prominence under the Nazis, and while most scholarship was not explicitly supportive of the regime, it had not been inimical to it either. After the war many Germanists were able to republish papers from the 1930s and 1940s simply by finding acceptable substitutes for compromised nouns and adjectives: "race" turned into "nation," "*völkisch*" became "national" or "ethnic," and "blood" and "tribes" (both of particular importance to Nazi literary scholarship) were converted into "tradition" and "regions." The generational rupture, then, was not only based on the intellectual obsolescence of traditional scholarship, but also in the impression that the latter was soiled by Nazism.

Under these circumstances it was a great deal more difficult for poststructuralism to acquire the radical stature that it quickly attained in the United States. To make matters worse, German critics were prone to raise two powerful objections which, ironically, were based on the premise that in the final analysis so-called French theory was a rather German affair. After all, who had been of greater importance to poststructuralist theorizing than Edmund Husserl, Sigmund Freud, Nietzsche, and, of course, Heidegger, without whom "Derrida and Lacan would be unthinkable" (Kittler 2000: 220). Moreover, the fact that the canonized German precursors had themselves sponged off earlier German contributions to critical thought served to further illuminate French theory's lack of originality. As Manfred Frank pointed out in his detailed inquiry *What is Neo-Structuralism?*, questions raised by Derrida and others regarding the mediation of reference and subjectivity by and through language had already been addressed and in part solved in the writings of Friedrich Schleiermacher (1768–1834) and other post-

Kantian Romantic hermeneutic philosophers. In short, what was good about French theory wasn't always that new, and what was new wasn't always that impressive.

But it was the closely related second objection that contributed in far greater measure to the acrimonious nature of the debate. Innocent observers may ask why the *German* base of French theory served to impede the latter's reception *in Germany*. The answer is simple: in the ideologically laced debates of the late sixties and early seventies indebtedness to Nietzsche and Heidegger was bound to encounter the ubiquitous *Irrationalismusvorwurf*, that is, the charge of irrationalism. Nietzsche – to summarize the accusation – had been a forerunner, Heidegger an enabler and erstwhile panegyrist of the Third Reich; hence poststructuralism's tendency to downplay history, eradicate the subject, and conjure up impersonal, determinist symbolic chains and networks was related to the ways in which National Socialism had mobilized and exploited the anti-rational tradition in German thought. Critics on the left saw the work of Derrida, Lacan, and Foucault as a kind of offshore laundering of politically compromised German theories that now, concealed underneath the fancy stylistics and terminological updating that the Parisian master thinkers excelled in, was poised to re-enter and re-poison young German minds. No wonder, then, that the early debates in Germany were at times far more acrimonious than in the United States; indeed North American journals like *Telos* (before it rode off in a very different political direction) were prone to translate German attacks on poststructuralist thought in order to pack a more powerful punch against the dubious French import (Lotringer and Cohen 2001: 138).

But like the heyday of Freiburg these theory squabbles are a thing of the past, as is Kittler's status as an outsider waging a guerrilla war against intellectual orthodoxies (and Kittler will occasionally indulge in retroactive self-dramatizations when talking about that bygone world of struggle). Nobody who holds a chair at the prestigious Humboldt University – politically cleansed after German reunification and striving to reconnect with its Wilhelmine glory days – is a rebel. Kittler's appointment in 1993 signaled that poststructuralism and media studies had ascended the academic ladder; and like most social climbers they did so by kicking others down a few rungs. Ironically, this promotion coincided with Kittler's growing distance from poststructuralism and media studies. We shall deal with that development in chapter 4; at this point, it will be helpful to briefly summarize how "1968" and the subsequent poststructuralist skirmishes shaped the attitude and approach of Kittler's earlier scholarship.

One of the more notorious polemical moves in Kittler's work is his tendency to indulge in drastically oversimplified accounts of the approaches and currents he disapproves of. Judging by his attacks, Germanic studies in the 1970s and 1980s was a hack job performed by hobby sociologists and amateurish activists on the left and by obsolete nineteenth-century humanists preaching timeless values and the glory of literature on the right, with a couple of clueless regurgitators of Freud thrown in between. This caricature is not only the outgrowth of heated debates that frequently deteriorated into ideological and personal mudslinging; it is also linked to the aforementioned point that for German readers familiar with the complexities of early hermeneutics, Heidegger's ontology of difference, and the conceptual subtleties of Adorno or Benjamin, the poststructuralist import did not have quite the innovative zest it enjoyed in the United States. It is only against the background of this caricature that the ideas of Foucault and Lacan appear as the decisive rupture that Kittler kept emphasizing. But if his academic peers had been as limited as he made them out to be, poststructuralism would indeed have been a revolutionary innovation.

This brings us back to Heidegger. There can be no doubt that of the many authorities and *maître penseurs* Kittler draws on – Hegel and Nietzsche, Lacan and Foucault, Turing and Shannon, McLuhan and Virilio – Heidegger is the most important. But while Kittler has in recent years been very outspoken about his admiration – "Nobody will ever get me to say a word against Heidegger" (Kittler 2003a: 84) – this wasn't the case earlier in his career. Heidegger is rarely mentioned or quoted before the 1990s. In his revealing interview with John Armitage, Kittler explains that as a student he deliberately avoided contact with Heidegger so as not to be overwhelmed: "[T]here were people that I knew whom Heidegger, who was retired at the time but whose presence and influence were ubiquitous, had broken, if not intentionally. I really knew people who, after an interview with Heidegger of just one hour, never finished their PhD because his questions and answers were so brilliant" (Armitage 2006: 20). Whether or not these dramatic stories of asphyxiation due to exposure to brilliance have any basis in fact is irrelevant; what is undoubtedly true is that virtually none of those who completed their projects and who came to think and write like Heidegger ever came up with anything that had not already been said by Heidegger. But the chances are that other reasons played into Kittler's reticence to approach "the little old man [. . .] shuffling along the corridors of the Freiburg philosophy department" (Kittler 2000: 220). For all his radical chic, the young Kittler was too ambitious and pragmatic not to realize that in the late 1960s deferential invocations of Heidegger would not augur well for a career as a Germanist. French poststructuralism offered a way out: "For me, the import of Foucault and Lacan rests on the fact that their writings allow possible ways of returning to Heidegger without naming him" (Armitage 2006: 20). As we shall see later, the older Kittler has moved closer to those who charge that French poststructuralism amounted to a rehashing of Heidegger. However, announcing this back in the early 1970s would not only have been politically inopportune, it would also have limited the revolutionary appeal of the new "poststructuralist" approach that Kittler was espousing. If Foucault and Lacan are reduced to francophone Heideggerian clones, if they are merely restating (albeit in more flowery prose) what Heidegger had already ruminated on, then there is no real innovation, no break, no rupture – which is precisely what the young Kittler and the rest of the marginalized German poststructuralist coterie were aiming at.

For one thing is clear and always has to be kept in mind when dealing with Kittler's more outlandish pronouncements: no matter how conservative he may appear, no matter how large the abyss that separates him from other German philosophers who gained prominence in the 1960s (starting with those linked to the Frankfurt School), Kittler has no doubt that his work and his obsessions are as much a part of "1968" as the more overtly political projects, and maybe even more so:

> Looking back, the 1960s are composed of many layers, one more hidden than the other, like neural networks in silicon or Freud's dreams. In the interest of presentability the year 1968 is immersed in the fireworks of fleeting student revolutions; on the next layer LPs are changed; then new beds are dawning; and on the penultimate layer there is the glimmer of new pills. The last one can no longer be retrieved. "This" – as the pirated editions of Freud's *Interpretation of Dreams* announced back then – "is the navel of the dream, the spot where it attaches to the unknown." (Kittler 2004: 199)

In other – and better-known – words, the cultural upheaval of the 1960s was not only a matter of politicking and street-fighting but also, and more fundamentally, of sex and drugs and rock 'n' roll. For Kittler, reading and analyzing Max Horkheimer and Theodor W. Adorno takes a back seat to listening to and analyzing Syd Barrett and Roger Waters. Ultimately, the world revolutions concocted in Berkeley or Vincennes are less important than the Beatles' "Revolution No. 9," engineered at Abbey Road. The reason for this sub-ordination of the political to the psychedelic is contained in the cryptic Freud reference quoted above: underlying all the political, musical, sexual, and drug-induced intoxications of the 1960s (or any other upheaval, for that matter) are dis-cursive and technological regimes which create and shape the so-called subjects who remain blissfully unaware of what makes them speak, think, and protest. To decipher these guiding structures and forces, to experience the intoxications of the day, *and then* to analyze them in technical detail is the real inheritance of the bygone cultural revolution. Together with Peter Sloterdijk's *Spheres* trilogy and Klaus Theweleit's ongoing *Pocahontas* and *King* projects (all of which strive to process the amorphous inheritance of the cultural upheavals of the sixties), Kittler's work should also be read as the last great drum roll of 1968.

But we should be wary of this exultation of bygone rebellions. No matter how extensive the ideological divide that separated and continues to separate Kittler from his politi-cally more progressive peers, they all appear to agree that "1968" was an upheaval that introduced something new. However, it is precisely this basic assumption – that is, the frequently unquestioned claim that the German student movement (whether armed with Marx or marijuana) struck a liberating blow against the vestiges of fascism, as well as against the authoritarian mindset of the 1950s with its stifling cultural conservatism – that has been called into in question. In a strident counterargument, the historian Götz Aly, himself a former student radical and now best known for his analyses of the links between the Holocaust and Nazi economic policy, has argued that the student movement was driven by deeply authoritarian impulses (Aly 2008). Despite their professed anti-authoritarianism, the rebellious students were ultimately more concerned with reinstating the clarity, order, and authority that Germany and the generation of their vanquished soldier-fathers had lost as a result of World War II. Nothing, Aly maintains, resembles the militant rhetoric of the progressive students of 1968 more than the militant rhetoric of the reactionary students of 1933, from the anti-bourgeois polemics and the preference for clearly circumscribed authentic collectives to the pervasive anti-Americanism and an occasionally pungent streak of anti-Semitism. (To tighten the screw, Aly entitled his book *Unser Kampf* or *Our Struggle*, an obvious reference to Hitler's *Mein Kampf*.) No doubt Kittler's exhibits certain authoritarian affects, be it the uncompromising discontent over the bourgeois vagaries of hermeneutical practice, the focus on the materialities of communication and their technological associations that mirrors the materialist focus on the economic base, or, as we shall discuss in chapter 4, a concern, couched in a certain anti-American rhetoric, that Germany should (re)regain a privileged position in the history of being.

History, Thomas Carlyle famously declared, is the essence of innumerable biographies. Like so many Victorian pronouncements, it profits from an inversion: biography emerges from innumerable histories. From the Stalingrad trauma to the cultural upheavals of 1968, from the theory reveries of Freiburg to the reunited Berlin, the vagaries of German twentieth-century history feed into Kittler's work.

Academic and boring as it may appear, his biography is shot through with the histories of war, upheavals, intoxications, and delusions that dominated the most troubled German century.

2

DISCOURSE ANALYSIS

1. FIRST TEASER: HERMENEUTIC HUSH-A-BYE

On the evening of September 7, 1780 – or 1783, the experts have yet to agree – Johann Wolfgang von Goethe scribbled eight lines on the wall of a mountain hermitage. The result, commonly referred to as "Wanderers Nachtlied" ("Wanderer's Nightsong"), is arguably the best of the shortest and the shortest of the best German poems (followed here by a deliberately pedestrian literal translation):

> *Über allen Gipfeln*
> *Ist Ruh,*
> *In allen Wipfeln*
> *Spürest du*
> *Kaum einen Hauch;*
> *Die Vögelein schweigen im Walde.*
> *Warte nur, balde*
> *Ruhest du auch.* (Goethe I, 1978: 142)

Above all mountain tops
Is calm,
In all tree tops
You feel
Hardly a breeze;
The little birds are quiet in the wood.
Just wait, soon
You will rest too.

This is a poem by Goethe, Germany's iconic man of letters, hence there is no lack of learned interpretations. While some readings emphasize the sociopolitical context, others descend into more profound depths:

There is in it not a simile, not a metaphor, not a symbol. Three brief, simple statements of fact are followed by a plain assertion for the future [. . .] We point to the immediacy with which language here conveys the hush of evening. [. . .] It is absolutely essential, it is indeed the heart of the poem's meaning and the feature which stamps it peculiarly and specifically Goethean, that *Gipfel* should precede *Wipfel.* For the order of the objects mentioned is not arbitrary. [. . .] It is an order of the inner process of nature as known by the mind, an organic order of the evolutionary progression in nature, from the inanimate to the animate, from the mineral, through the vegetable, to the animal kingdom [. . .] and so inevitably to man. A natural process [. . .] has become language, has been wrought in another substance, the poet's own material [. . .] It would be difficult to find in literature a lyric of such brevity containing so much profundity of objective thought. (Wilkinson; quoted in Goethe I, 1978: 544–5)

This is such an impressive animal-vegetable-mineral interpretation that it was considered worthy of inclusion – in its
original English, no less – in the commentary section of the
esteemed Hamburg edition of Goethe's works. No doubt
the poem invites such readings. The "inner process" that
seamlessly ties together the various inanimate and animate
regions of nature is engineered by the skillful deployment
of words that cover a wide semantic expanse. Note Goethe's
use of *Hauch*, a poetically charged noun that means both
(animate) breath and (inanimate) breeze, or of the verb *ruhen*
which can refer to all states of rest from eternal slumber to
an afternoon nap. Moving down to the sub-lexical level, Emil
Staiger, one of the twentieth century's leading Germanists,
stressed how in the poem's first two lines "the long 'u' and
the pause following it make the silent twilight audible," and
how the *du* in line four "is not as profoundly calming because
the sentence does not end and the voice remains raised, and
this corresponds to the last faint rustling in the trees" (1991:
41). Without any bumps or friction, the poem glides across
nature to man, gracefully merging mountains, trees, birds,
and wanderers; it soothes and cocoons readers with its seamless transition from the vowel *u* to *du* ('thou') and *Ruh* ('rest')
and from there on to the assurance that even the most inac-
cessible alpine and arboreal regions are eager to calm "that
most restless of beings, man" (Staiger 1991: 42).

In 1979 Kittler published a reading of "Wanderer's
Nightsong," entitled "Lullaby in Birdland." (Kittler belongs
to a select group of German academics who enjoy English
titles, especially those alluding to technology and/or popular
culture; though it is doubtful whether many of his colleagues
caught the reference to Charlie Parker.) While not overly
troubled by the restless state of man, Kittler readily admits
that analyses such as Staiger's describe the linguistic tricks
and effects of Goethe's poem well; however, they ignore

the discursive preconditions that enabled the poem to operate in such a way. Meaning and meter alone do not account for its effect. How does language have to be constituted for the poem to cast its spell? What order of discourse, what mechanisms of speech production, what rituals of language acquisition have to be in place in order to lure the wanderer and his readers into an "audible twilight" in which trees and mountains are brimming with soothing messages and in which even the absence of bird chatter is full of spiritual significance? Kittler is less interested in what the poem is saying than in uncovering the mechanisms that produce meaning in the first place.

He starts out with one of the most threadbare questions of traditional criticism: *Wer spricht* – who is speaking? As the conspicuous use of the pronoun *du* indicates, the "discursive event" (1991: 106) of the poem is an interpellation. A voice is addressing the wanderer; more precisely: a voice is speaking to the wanderer of the ways in which nature is speaking to him, with the result that the wanderer (and his readers) cannot but interpret even the most meaningless noise as a meaningful message. So who is speaking? To cut to the core of Kittler's analysis, it is the voice of the *mother*. This may sound quaintly Freudian, yet it is crucial to understand that Kittler is not providing a trite psychoanalytic reading. Instead he delivers an analysis of an incisive rupture in the order of speech that gave rise to Goethe's poem and subsequently to Freud's psychoanalysis. The poem is not read through Freud; if Freud is of any importance at all, he is read through the poem.

In the second half of the eighteenth century the upbringing of infants and children underwent significant changes. The emergence of the bourgeois nuclear family with its near-total relegation of women to the private sphere redefined and promoted the role of the mother as the principal caregiver. Breaking with practices that were common in the extended families of the Middle Ages and the Early Modern Age, mothers were now charged with turning raw infant material into individuals equipped with a sufficiently developed psychic center of resonance and reflexivity, commonly referred to as spirit or soul. This required that mothers be taught how to teach their children. Within a short period a wide array of new child-rearing practices emerged. For instance, when it came to putting babies to sleep, herbal concoctions, sedatives, tranquilizers, narcotics, and other barbarian means which treated the infant as nothing more than a "a body among bodies" (Kittler 1991: 198) gave way to the loving voice of the mother singing lullabies. Goethe's tree-top poem, Kittler argues, is based on an old lullaby from Saxony, but far more importantly it re-creates the salient features of the voice of the mother, thus triggering in the wanderer and, by extension, in hermeneutically conditioned readers a response similar to that of an infant listening to *Hush-a-bye-Baby on the Tree Top*. To introduce a phrase that will recur several times, Goethe's poem is a "discourse on discourse channel conditions" (Kittler 1982: 473); it foregrounds and performs the rules, codes, and cultural ruptures which allow it to affect its readers.

But how exactly did this effect come about? In a detailed analysis in *Discourse Networks*, Kittler analyzes how in the latter part of the eighteenth century education reformers brought about a substantial change in language-teaching practices (1990: 27–53). Having children pick up language by listening to unwieldy biblical names or strings of letters or phonemes became a thing of the past. Instead mothers were instructed to voice what Kittler calls "minimal signifieds," such as *du mu bu be ma am ag ga*. These are neither real words (though some of them – for instance, *am* or *du* – can indeed be words) nor meaningless syllables, but located somewhere in the middle. What is important is their ability to naturally merge into words: *bu* and *be* result in *Bube* (little boy), a simple repetition of *ma* yields *Mama*. "In this way meanings come into being on the border between sound and word through the augmentation of minimal signifieds" (Kittler 1990: 78). The effortless fusion is based on the assumption that minimal signifieds like *bu*, *be*, or *ma* are always already pregnant with meaning. In defiance of common linguistic wisdom meaning is already present on the sub-lexical level. This assumption is reinforced by the new and intimate bond between mother and infant, for the latter will perceive the voice of the former as always being directed toward something. Together, the love of the mother and the semantic plenitude of language guarantee that whatever comes out of the mother's mouth will and must be meaningful. We are dealing with nothing less than the discursive construction – propagated by poets, philosophers, and education reformers – of that particular type of intimate, eroticized motherhood which 100 years later will be excavated by Freud and presented as a near-universal constant.

This "methodological purification of speech" (Kittler 1990: 37) was one of the most important elements of a cultural rupture in the course of which language fundamentally changed its status. Seamlessly growing out of quasi-natural basic constituents, language became a "general, purified, homogenous medium" (1990: 36). As a result, language, nature, and the voice of the mother are all meaning and no noise. How, then, can a poem by Goethe that re-mediates a maternal lullaby in order to conjure up the meaning of nature not be full of meaning? Just as the child perceives the mother's minimal signifieds to be pregnant with meaning, Goethe's wanderer perceives even the most meaningless natural sound to be brimming with existential significance, and sufficiently alphabetized readers perceive the 8 lines, 24 words, and 155 characters of Goethe's poem to be bursting with hermeneutically accessible riches. The poem both describes and brings about a hermeneutic infection precisely because it re-stages that which made us susceptible to this type of infection in the first place. The medium – Goethe's enchanting artifact of words – is the message.

2. REWIRING THE FRENCH CONNECTION

Let us step back for a moment. Underlying this reading of "Wanderer's Nightsong" are two premises with large-scale implications that will continue to guide Kittler's work for most of his career: *the disempowerment of the speaking subject* and *the discontinuity of the orders of speech*.

1. Kittler's analysis presupposes that we are not masters of our language. Language was there before us, we grew up surrounded by it, we grew *into* it, it colonized us – whatever "us" was before it was framed, carved up, and identified by language. Language provided the basic distinctions which are commonly said to precede it. It is through the deferring structure of language (a word stands in for something, thus both distancing and conjuring up the latter) that we apprehend the basic mechanisms of deferral, substitution, and desire. It is through language that we gain our sense of identity as separate entities, for what was "I" at first other than something that was called "you" by someone else? We do not speak language as much as language speaks us. To phrase it in the shortest way possible, language *subjects* us. This linguistic disempowerment of man, the alleged master of language, is indebted to the structuralist psychoanalysis of Lacan. Rewriting Freud (while claiming to spell out what Freud really meant), Lacan argued that the subconscious was structured like a language because its emergence was tied to the subject being immersed in the symbolic structure of language.

2. The second premise is that history is subject to incisive cultural breaks. The so-called Discourse Network 1800 (roughly, from the later eighteenth to the mid- nineteenth century) is completely distinct from the so-called Scholar's Republic that came before; and it is separated by an equally radical caesura from the Discourse Network 1900 that arrived with new analog media technologies in the second half of the nineteenth century. So incisive are these ruptures that they preclude the usual cultural continuities. There is no tradition, no discernible cultural trajectory, no red thread or grand narrative (be it of progress and emancipation or of decadence and decline) that runs through the breaks. If the subordination of the subject to the symbolic grid of language comes courtesy of Lacan, this dramatic history of caesuras is indebted to Foucault, more precisely (given that Foucault was different things at different times), to the discourse-analytical or "archeological" Foucault of the mid-1960s. In *The Order of Things*, his "most elegant book" (Kittler 2003a: 38), Foucault described a sequence of epochs, each of which was ruled by an episteme "that defines the conditions of possibility of all knowledge, whether expressed in a theory or silently invested in a practice" (Foucault 1994: 168). The focus is not on varying belief systems but on the underlying ordering principles of knowledge. Once the basic orders of discourse change, even the most venerable red threads or timeless props of history disintegrate. The "almost uninterrupted development of the European ratio from Renaissance to our own day," Foucault remarked, is "only a surface appearance; on the archeological level we see that the system of positivities was transformed in a wholesale fashion at the end of the eighteenth and the beginning of the nineteenth century" (1994: xxii). This rupturism is inherited by Kittler: "The historical adventures of speaking do not form a continuum and so do not constitute a history of

ideas" (1990: 177). Rather, they constitute – to anticipate our final chapters – what Heidegger called a "history of being" (*Seinsgeschichte*), a succession of fundamentally different ways in which humans relate to being. The specifically Kittlerian twist is the merging of these two premises. Foucault is lacanized, Lacan is foucaultized. With the help of Lacan, Foucault's discourse analysis or archeology is equipped with a psychoanalytic extension in order to show how discursive regimes shape the unconscious by inscribing, for instance, subject positions within the new familial order. With the help of Foucault, Lacan's unhistorical analysis is historicized in order to show that psychic inscription processes undergo radical shifts in time. Foucault's epistemes are not only involved in the formation of knowledge but also in that of the human psyche; Lacan's discourse is made far more concrete by excavating its different historical instantiations. "[T]he term *discourse* no longer refers, as in Lacan's rendering, to the linguistic and therefore abstract notion of extended speech, but rather to positive modes of existence of language as shaped by institutions of pedagogy, technical means of reproduction, storage and transfer, available strategies of interpretation, and so on" (Wellbery 1990: xxi). Disempowerment and discontinuity: people are shaped and inscribed by a priori discursive regimes, but in time the latter undergo such fundamental changes that it requires a considerable amount of blindness to shape them into a coherent grand narrative.

The provocative dimension of this French connection arises from two scandalous features (scandalous, that is, in the 1960s). First, while Foucault meticulously dissected various epistemes, he neither explained why they arose nor how they managed to maintain themselves. Not only did he summarily dismiss the traditional key players at the center of modern history (the transcendental subject, the middle class, capitalism, the spread of enlightenment, the perfection of society, the nation-state, and all the other usual suspects), but he also denied that it was possible to fully account for the theories, ideologies, belief systems, or aesthetic products of any given age by referring them to their social context or carriers:

> [T]hough membership of a social group can always explain why such and such a person chose one system of thought rather than another, the condition enabling that one system of thought never resided in the existence of the group. We must be careful to distinguish here between two forms and two levels of investigation. The first would be a study of opinions [. . .] The other, which takes no account of the persons involved, or their history, consists in defining the conditions on the basis of which it was possible to conceive of [. . .] knowledge [. . .] The first analysis would be the province of a doxology. Archeology can recognize and practise only the second. (Foucault 1994: 200)

The first scandal had less to do with Foucault's claim that the differences between epistemes were so vast as to preclude all talk of intellectual continuity or progress than with the fact that he had the gall to highlight a period of wholesale transition at the end of the eighteenth and the beginning of the nineteenth century (in fact, he singled out the year 1795 as particularly important) without any reference to what was going on in society. With the courage of impudence, Foucault dared *not* to speak of the French Revolution. Kittler inherits this rupturism as well as the provocative disdain for social or contextual explanations. The Foucault of the mid-sixties and the early seventies in France and the Kittler of the late seventies and early eighties in Germany are simultaneously shooting at the left and at the right. The right is snubbed by the dismissal of any and all references to cultural continuities and traditional values, not to mention the disdain for the fundamentals of hermeneutic scholarship popular among more conservative scholars. The left is snubbed by the equally insolent dismissal of any and all references to societal structures or economic contexts, not to mention the disdain for grand historical narratives of progressive or even revolutionary enlightenment popular among left-wing scholars. This two-front war is made easier by the fact that for Foucault as well as for Kittler there is not that much difference between left and right to begin with. Of course, there are exceptions on both sides of the political spectrum, but most approaches – according to the poststructuralist diagnosis – remain spellbound by notions of cultural continuity that, in one way or another, are all rooted in the conceptualization of humans as vessels of timeless values or as the yet-to-be-fully-realized subjects of history. In a word, both Foucault and Kittler are taking aim at the belief that there is, was, and will be something called *l'homme*, *der Mensch* or "man."

This is the second scandal: the very explicit anti-humanism emerging from the archeological diagnosis that man-the-subject is a discursive construct that first appeared in the late eighteenth century as a result of the modern arrangements of knowledge. An array of sciences appears that places man at the center of all intellectual endeavor. But "man is neither the oldest nor the most constant problem that has been posed for human knowledge," Foucault reminded his readers, "man is an invention of recent date" (1994: 386). Not only is man young, he is already nearing his end, as Foucault pointed out in the most notorious prediction of cultural theory since Nietzsche's closely related proclamation that God is dead:

If those arrangements were to disappear as they appeared, if some event of which we can at the moment do no more than sense the possibility – without knowing either what its form will be or what it promises – were to cause them to crumble, as the ground of classical thought did, at the end of the eighteenth century, then one can certainly wager that man would be erased, like a face drawn in sand at the edge of the sea. (Foucault 1994: 387)

We will return to this quote since one of the basic messages of Kittler's work is that the event obliquely referred to by Foucault has already taken place. As we shall see, Kittler has figured out the nature and the location of the beach that witnessed the disappearance of man's image. He also knows when and how that image came about in the first place. But while Foucault pursued an archeology of the sciences, Kittler's insight is based primarily on the discourse analysis or archeology of literary texts that acted as inscription techniques for the creation of the modern subject. Goethe's "Wanderer's Nightsong" revealed and romanticized one of the most elementary techniques involved in this project. Though it is just as easy to speculate that it also hints at man's coming demise:

Warte nur, balde
Ruhest du auch.

Just wait, soon
You will rest too.

3. KISS OF THE SNAKE WOMAN: THE BIRTH OF POETRY AND PHILOSOPHY FROM THE SPIRIT(S) OF BUREAUCRACY

Kittler defines discourse networks as "the network of technologies and institutions that allow a given culture to select, store and process relevant data" (1990: 369). A culture is a large-scale information machine which, depending on the way the data inputs, throughputs, and outputs are wired, produces basic notions as to why and to what end this machinery is supposed to function. One of the most persistent notions is the claim that culture is, somehow, tied to human significance. Culture may reveal the essence of humanity, act as a harbinger for human ideals, or indicate what "man" is or could or should be; at the very least, culture expresses the allegedly uniquely human gift of recognizing, providing, and processing the significance of objects and artifacts beyond their most basic appearance and/or use value. No culture insisted more strongly on this humanist belief than that which emerged out of the Discourse Network 1800. Of course, it did not only come about as a result of changing language acquisition practices re-created in Goethe's poem. They were no more than a part of a linked network of cultural techniques, ranging from the reform of writing lessons all the way to the new hermeneutical practices of the newly promoted disciplines of philosophy and aesthetics, and, last but certainly not least, to the bureaucratic reforms designed to mobilize and install modern, self-reflexive, and self-directing subjects as civil servants in the service of the emerging nation-state. At the center, however, are those cultural techniques that concern the speaking, writing, and reading of language.

The analysis is not easy, to say the least. *Discourse Networks* is, in the modest self-appraisal of its author, "a damned learned book" (Kittler and Weinberger 2009: 94). Large portions of the first half, detailing the Discourse Network 1800, require a graduate level of intimacy with German literature. We can leave out a lot because it is of little relevance for students of media and communication, but in order to single out the important aspects it is helpful to make use of a literary backdoor. Kittler himself endorses this strategy by placing in the middle of his own analysis a reading of E. T. A. Hoffmann's famous fairy tale "The Golden Pot" (1990: 77–108), a tale he claims to have interpreted "better than many others" (Kittler and Weinberger 2009: 94). Indeed, those keen on understanding the first half of *Discourse Networks* are advised to start by enjoying Hoffmann's tale before tackling Kittler.

At the center of the story is the handsome yet accident-prone student Anselmus who, after toppling over a basket full of apples belonging to an angry witch and forfeiting what little money he has, withdraws underneath an elder tree on the banks of the River Elbe to bemoan his unhappy fate. Were it not for his clumsiness, Anselmus would successfully pursue an administrative career and maybe even rise to the lofty heights of a Privy Councilor. In other words, he could be a high-ranking Prussian civil servant if only he stopped spilling ink, missing appointments, and slipping on side-walks. But now Anselmus has a life-changing experience. His soliloquy is interrupted

> by a singular rustling and crackling which began near him in the grass, but which soon glided up into the leaves and branches of the elder tree spreading over his head. First it seemed as if an evening breeze were shaking the leaves, then as if little birds were twittering on the branches, their small wings mischievously fluttering to and fro. Then a whisper-ing and a lisping began, and it seemed as if the sound of little crystal bells was coming from the blossoms. Anselmus listened and listened. Then – he himself knew not how – the whispering and the lisping and the tinkling turned into half-heard words:
>
> "Betwixt, between, betwixt the branches, between the blossoms, shooting, twisting, twirling we come! Sister, sister, swing in the shimmer – quickly, quickly, in and out,

Rays of sunset, whispering wind of the evening, sounds of dew, singing blossoms – we sing with the branches and the blossoms; stars soon to sparkle – we must descend; betwixt, between, twisting, turning, swirling. Sisters we!" (Hoffmann 1969: 63–4)

Three gold-green snakes appear, one of whom fixes her "marvelous blue eyes" with "unspeakable desire" on Anselmus who straightaway falls in love. Elder tree, wind, and sunlight start talking to him, pointing out that it is due to his newfound feelings that he is able to understand them: love has turned shade, breath, and light into comprehendible speech. Suddenly a paternal male voice orders the snakes home, and to the amazement of passers-by Anselmus is left clutching the elder tree, pining for his vanished ophidian object of desire.

The amorous snake in question, Serpentina, boasts an interesting pedigree. Her father is at one and the same time the highly respected though somewhat odd Royal Archivarius Lindhorst, a keeper of old manuscripts, and a mighty "Prince of Spirits," a magic fire salamander exiled from the Empire of Atlantis until he can marry off his three daughters to men with a "childlike poetic nature" (Hoffmann 1969: 111). Anselmus, a poet at heart, fits the bill. In order to test his future son-in-law's worthiness, Lindhorst (true to his reptilian provenance, his name roughly translates as "dragon's lair") hires him to copy old manuscripts, including an Arabic script and then a more mysterious parchment of "exotic characters" referred to as *Bhagavad-Gita*'s masters" (Hoffmann 1969: 105). Despite his calligraphic training, the bumbling Anselmus would hardly be up to the task were it not for the appearance of Serpentina, this time in human shape, whose caresses and loving words of encouragement help him along. It is only when Anselmus, under the influence of Lindhorst's enemies, starts to doubt the magic identity of his employer, as well as the very existence of Serpentina, that the strange characters become so illegible as to be uncopyable. Their "crabbed strokes and twirls" look like "a piece of thickly veined marble, or a stone which had been sprinkled with mosses" (Hoffmann 1969: 119). But in the end – after Hoffmann's trademark mix of magical burlesque and philistine slapstick – love conquers all and Anselmus and Serpentina retire in conjugal bliss to Atlantis, a spiritual realm that Lindhorst describes as "life in poetry, poetry to which the sacred harmony of all things is revealed as the most profound secret of Nature" (Hoffmann 1969: 136).

The opening scene on the banks of the Elbe depicts an experience similar to that of Goethe's weary wanderer. Rustling and crackling change into whispering and lisping which then magically transform into "half-heard words." The snakes' song, in turn, graduates from rhythmic onomatopoeia emulating their twisting motion to well-phrased poetic discourse. Hoffmann's tale makes explicit what in the case of Goethe's poem had to be unearthed by archeological analysis: it is the voice of Woman or Love or Nature – which in the Discourse Network 1800 were synonymous (Kittler 1990: 73) – that enables the seamless transition from noise to sound to speech. Love makes trees and reptiles speak in and with human tongues. The same applies to writing. Were it not for Serpentina, Anselmus would be faced either with meaningless natural phenomena (veined marble or moss-covered rock) or with equally illegible alien scripts (Arabic). However, inspired by love, he is not only able to effortlessly reproduce Lindhorst's mysterious manuscripts, but audibly understands what he is writing. While copying the strange story of Lindhorst's previous life and banishment, Anselmus hears the very words he is reproducing voiced by Serpentina.

Once again, a seamless continuity from nature to culture is established; and, once again, Kittler ties it to changes in language instruction. Just as the new language acquisition practices taught children to merge minimal signifieds into words, the new writing lessons taught them to merge the basic strokes (vertical lines, half-circles, half-ovals) into letters and then words which are "naturally" understood and heard. This is precisely what happens in Hoffmann's tales. The writing scenes in *The Golden Pot* "put a simple school program into practice" (Kittler 1990: 97); they show how what we read and write is always already heard and seen. Whether manipulated by quills or tongues, meaningless constituent elements are combined into meaningful units; and humans inscribed by these cultural techniques will come to believe that nothing is meaningless because everything is always already on the threshold of meaning. Beyond this guarantee of constant semantic plenitude, the most momentous consequence of the new pedagogical techniques described by Kittler was the emergence of the modern subject:

> Whoever wrote in block letters would not be an in-dividual [*sic*] [. . .] The great metaphysical unities invented in the age of Goethe – the developmental process of *Bildung*, autobiography, world history – could be seen as the flow of the continuous and the organic simply because they were supported by flowing, cursive handwriting [. . .] To develop handwriting as out of one mold means to produce individuals. (Kittler 1990: 83–4).

The adverb *simply* in the quote above is vintage Kittlerese (more of which in the concluding chapter), but it should be noted that Kittler is – simply or not – rephrasing what in more stately fashion had been diagnosed by the philosopher Hegel:

Thus, if at first the specific nature and innate peculiarity of the individual, together with what these become as a result of cultivation and education, are taken as the inner, as the essence of his action and his fate, then this essence has its appearance and externality to begin with in his mouth, hand, voice, handwriting, and the other organs and their permanent characteristics. Thereafter, and not till then, does it give itself further outward expression in its actual existence in the world. (Hegel 1977: 189–90)

Kittler's analysis updates Hegel by inverting him. Handwriting is not the external appearance of an already present inner individual; on the contrary, the inner essence came about by the training of "mouth, hand, voice, handwriting." In short, the emergence of subject, soul, and spirit (*Geist*), all the ineffable qualities that signify Foucault's metaphysically burdened man, *is tied to changes in the materialities of communication*. Where letters were, there subjects shall be.

In the closed circuits of the Discourse Network 1800, the modern male individual receives language from Woman (be it the empirical mother or any loving Serpentina), but since Nature or Woman do not speak clearly it will be up to the male subjects, once they have been taught to write by their fathers or paternal authority figures like Lindhorst, to translate the discourse of Woman or Nature into poetry and literature. This output, in turn, will be read, first, by many female readers who thereby will learn how to speak and thus be able to teach language, and, second, by philosophers like Hegel, who, banking on the guarantee of meaningfulness that permeates the system, will provide the metaphysical legitimation for the subject that arises from the new pedagogical and literary practices. The Discourse Network 1800 is based on "an endless oscillating from Nature to books and back to Nature" (Kittler 1990: 91).

There is no doubt something mechanical about these circuits of speaking, writing, and reading; indeed Kittler himself has described the Discourse Network 1800 as well as his analysis of it as a grand information machine:

> Basically, I linearized the history of Mothers, Poetry and Philosophy around 1800: the mother generates the mass of words which literature takes over and turns into works, and philosophy rereads the entire output of this production as theory. I visualized the whole thing as a switchboard diagram, which explains why technological metaphors like "feedback" started cropping up. But it was supposed to be more than a matter of mere metaphors, I wanted to structure entire blocks of the text in his way. So I really took care that the Mother enters the channel of Poetry as input and, upon exiting at the other side, is collected in the storage medium of Philosophy. That was the concept. From the beginning, the book was designed like a machine. (Kittler and Banz 1996: 45)

And that is precisely what discourse networks are: a set of large-scale, historically contingent information machines, one of which gained particular prominence by producing cultural entities such as the new nuclear family, composed of modern subjects equipped with the requisite hermeneutical skills.

4. YOU MUST REMEMBER THIS: HERETIC GERMAN LESSONS

At this point readers not familiar with Kittler (and possibly some who are) may feel inclined to share the frequent charges leveled at the counterintuitive, idiosyncratic, or downright bizarre nature of his arguments. No doubt his elliptical style and his penchant for provocation cater to these objections. However, almost three decades after the initial publication of *Discourse Networks* and related earlier works, and two decades after the heated theory wars of the eighties have subsided, it is becoming clear how close Kittler is to some of the most established and orthodox ideas of German studies. Three important points stand out:

1. Most scholars agree that the late eighteenth-century irruption of German literature onto the world stage could not have come about without the work of Protestant clergymen and their (frequently prodigal) sons. "The Protestant pastor is the grandfather of German philosophy," Nietzsche – himself the prodigal son of a Protestant clergyman – mocked (Nietzsche 2002: 24). He is also the father of German literature. If Paris bred French literature, German literature came of age in a country parsonage. "It has been calculated that, even excluding philosophers, 120 major literary figures writing in German and born between 1676 and 1804 had either studied theology or were the children of Protestant pastors" (Boyle 2008: 10).

The hallmark of this cultural tradition is said to be *Innerlichkeit*. Usually translated as interiority or inwardness, *Innerlichkeit* is tied to the secularization of Protestant and Pietist soul-searching and self-observation practices that involved probing and verbalizing one's feelings towards God. Especially in the second half of the enlightened eighteenth century, the richly developed religious lexicon that suffused German parsonages was extracted from its religious origins and increasingly applied to nature and to other human beings. The plus side was an impressive psychological expertise and a keen eye for the processes of subject formation (as evident in the German *Bildungsroman*), as well as a profound awareness of the problems of consciousness, self-reflexivity, and communication that reached its zenith in the idealist philosophy of Schelling, Fichte, and Hegel (and that enjoyed a late blooming in Niklas Luhmann's systems theory). The flip side was a marked negligence for the more mundane matters of the world, including the political, social, and economic spheres that received far more attention in English or French literature. Kittler's archeology of the hermeneutical enrichment of language brought about by new pedagogical acquisition and philosophical interpretation practices, then, represents an interesting twist on this secularization and refunctionalization of religious discourse. The conventional approach to German cultural history claims that the plenitude of meaning that was initially guaranteed by God is subsequently applied to nature and interpersonal relationships (which is why it is in many instances difficult to tell whether poems by Goethe and his contemporaries are addressed to God, Jesus, the German forests, or a German girl). In Kittler's account the same plenitude of meaning was first guaranteed not by any divine force but by the natural origin of language emanating from the "mother's mouth."

2. While this highly influential refunctionalization of religious discourse for literary and philosophical purposes is a fairly German affair, the familial setting is not. The new child-rearing and language-teaching practices Kittler focuses on were part of a momentous shift that affected many Western societies on the verge of the Industrial Revolution and that created the alleged unconscious universals later excavated by Freud. It was accompanied by the growing middle-class rift between a public and private sphere that relegated women to the latter. Kittler is aware of this, but rather than discuss the socio-economic developments triggered by capitalism gathering steam (literally and metaphorically), he restricts himself to discursive practices. The net result, however, appears to be the same: as muses and mothers who inspire and provide the input, and as readers and consumers who

pore over the aesthetic output, the middle-class women of Kittler's Discourse Network 1800 are as excluded from *cultural* production as they are in the standard socio-historical accounts from *material* production.

3. But, even in combination with the differentiation into public and private spheres, the secularization of religious discourse does not fully explain the frequently commented upon apolitical, "unworldy," and indeed slightly provincial appearance of much eighteenth- and nineteenth-century German literature. Any first-year student of German studies can explain the latter: dispersed across a patchwork of kingdoms, dukedoms, petty principalities, and city-states, the German middle class was economically under-developed and politically fragmented; whatever energies it had were channeled (as in the case of Anselmus) primarily into administrative and intellectual pursuits. While the British bourgeoisie set sail to create and exploit an empire, and their French counterpart took to the streets to stage a revolution, the economically and politically atrophied German middle class congregated in governmental offices and lecture halls to pursue empires and revolutions of the mind. Heinrich Heine's famous remarks – that "German philosophy is nothing but the dream of the French Revolution" (Heine 2006: 246) and that Kant's philosophical guillotine, decapitating unwarranted metaphysical speculation, represents the equivalent of Robespierre's guillotine decimating political opponents – are as politically perceptive as they are historically and philosophically astute. The common perception seems to be that the French act while the Germans merely think. (Not surprisingly, it was not uncommon among educated nineteenth- and twentieth-century Germans to subsequently claim that it is more honorable to be German and to understand things you are not fully able to do than to be French and do things you do not fully understand.) But even though Kittler studiously

avoids any reference to the basics of German socio-economic history (just as Foucault provocatively withheld any homage to the French Revolution), his narrative nonetheless ends up telling much the same story. The renowned apex of German cultural production – the literature of classicism and Romanticism, from Goethe and Schiller to Hoffmann and Hölderlin, the heights of philosophic speculation that climax in Hegel and Clausewitz, the contributions of the Grimms and the Humboldts – is not the result of the economic ascendance of property-owning budding entrepreneurs but the work of state officials, governmental clerks, and publicly employed academics. While the conventional accounts focus on how the middle class was forced into these bureaucracies, Kittler centers on the techniques that equipped these bureaucracies with expansive hermeneutic expertise.

It is the ideal union of poet and bureaucrat, so memorably embodied by Goethe (and ironically romanticized in Hoffmann's semi-reptilian librarian Lindhorst), that becomes the real protagonist of the Discourse Network 1800. While Kittler never explicitly states that the technologies of subject formation and the new insistence on self-reflexivity directly came about in the service of the state, he clearly indicates that there was an ongoing feedback between the hermeneutics of state and subject. Changing discursive practices breed a literature of and for subjects, while the state breeds an administrative class of and for subjects. And once again it is Hegel, who in Kittler's narrative acts as the grand impresario of the Discourse Network 1800, who provides a philosophically informed reading of the cultural output: the final framework of the self-reflective subject (who stands in and provides a basis for the absolute spirit) is at this stage in history only possible within the framework of the (Prussian) state. The promise of love and meaning – which in the words of "The Golden Pot" entails the poetical recognition of "the sacred harmony of all things" – is fully embodied in the existence of the civil servant.

When read against the standard approaches to German history, then, Kittler's analysis of the Discourse Network 1800 amounts to a sequence of intriguing substitutes. Others ponder the redirection of religious discourse; he probes the eroticized discursive infections emanating from the "Mother's Mouth." Others focus on the public/private split with its attendant gender differentiation; he foregrounds the new language acquisition practices of the mother–child dyad. Others trace the migration of a socio-economically and politically hamstrung middle class into governmental administration and university careers; he highlights the philosophically embellished hermeneutic imperialism of poet-bureaucrats. The young Kittler, in short, was less of a rebel than a heretic. He was not introducing altogether new ideas but retelling old stories from a new angle. It soon became apparent, however, that the new angle needed a footing. In what remains his most influential move, Kittler began to ground discursive regimes in *media*.

3

MEDIA THEORY

1. SECOND TEASER: SYD'S SONG

Nietzsche, the renegade philologist and aspiring composer, was addicted to music. *Thus Spoke Zarathustra*, he claimed, may be classified as music, and music was at the heart of his first book, *The Birth of Tragedy from the Spirit of Music*, which effectively destroyed his professional standing as a professor of classical philology. The same is true of Kittler, the renegade philologist and aspiring student of modern recording technology. He too has repeatedly stressed the fundamental importance of music – and of rock music in particular – for his work. At the beginning of *Discourse Networks*, he writes, "stood the Fugs with their song 'Exorcising the Evil Spirits from the Pentagon'" (1990: 372; title corrected); the collection *Dichter Mutter Kind* ("Poet Mother Child") contains the entire score (including lyrics) of The Doors' *Apocalypse Now* anthem "The End" (1991: 99–103); and with his most recent project, *Musik und Mathematik*, Kittler ends up where

Nietzsche started, in ancient Greece surrounded by music, though it remains to be seen whether Kittler's latest books will be as damaging to his academic reputation as Nietzsche's first was to his. But with the possible exception of Wagner's operas – another passion Kittler shares with Nietzsche – no music has had the same impact on him as that of Pink Floyd. Their lyrics already appear as mottos in his dissertation (Kittler 1977: 26 and 161); thirty years later they provide chapter headings for *Musik und Mathematik* (Kittler 2006a: 43). In the German academic habitat of the late 1970s and early 1980s it was still considered a breach of etiquette to take rock music this seriously; in fact Kittler's habit of making Pink Floyd LPs part of his bibliographic apparatus was later cited as an example of the poststructuralist erosion of the boundary between scholarly and literary discourse. But the high point of Kittler's engagement with "the Pinks [*sic*]" (Kittler and Maresch 1994: 95) occurred in 1982, with his analysis of one of their best-known songs, "Brain Damage," from the 1973 album *Dark Side of the Moon* (Kittler 1982).

Goethe and Pink Floyd are rarely mentioned in one breath but for the following it is interesting to note that "Brain Damage" is not that dissimilar from "Wanderer's Nightsong." Once again sounds and voices impact a solitary listener; once again this impact proceeds along clearly defined stages (mountains and trees in Goethe's poem; meadows and corridors in "Brain Damage"); and once again it is ultimately not quite clear who ends up speaking or singing to whom inside whose head. Most importantly, Kittler once again sidelines the usual interpretations – the song is about angst, alienation, or our inability to respond to "the child" or "the real human being living inside" (Roger Waters, quoted in Jones 1996: 101) – in favor of an analytical shift from the inside to the outside, from human truths and messages to rules, conditions, and (technical) standards. In much the same way as he had handled Goethe's poem, Kittler treats "Brain Damage" not as a song that requires interpretation but as a "discourse on discourse channel conditions" (Kittler 1982: 473). He analyzes "Brain Damage" as a highly seductive techno-acoustic event – one whose seductive qualities arise from a sophisticated and self-conscious performance of advances in sound technology. Indeed, "Brain Damage" is said to retrace and perform the history of recording technology; it is nothing less than a musically staged genealogy of rock music that manages to link its self-performance to the question of how technology relates to madness.

In the first stanza "the loonies" are outside "on the grass," their distant voices and laughter are so far removed from the listener that they cannot be spatially localized. "As an acoustic quote, then, the first stanza is the meagre time of monaural reproduction" (1982: 471). In the second stanza, however, the lunatics are the in the hall, which is specified as "my hall":

> Already by virtue of the possessive pronoun there is a defined spatial relationship between the hall and the voice that is listening and speaking. The hall is near enough to allow for an acoustic differentiation between left and right, between one and many lunatics. This is exactly how at the end of *Grantchester Meadows* the acoustically built staircase functions, on which steps proceed from left to right – from vinyl directly in rooms and into the ears of the listeners. Stanza two, then, is the time of High Fidelity and stereophony. (1982: 471–72)

Finally, "the lunatic is in my head." Due to further advances in sound reproduction, sounds and voices coming from all angles surround and invade the listener. This is primarily due to the invention of the "Azimuth Coordinator," an acoustic irradiation device Kittler mistakenly attributes to Syd Barrett (1946–2006), the founding member and first leader of Pink Floyd, but which was in fact "essentially a crude pan pot device made by Bernard Speight, an Abbey Road technical engineer, using four large rheostats which were converted from 270 degree rotation to 90 degree" (Cunningham). In combination with a rudimentary quadraphonic PA system – in plain English, a couple of extra speakers set up around the room – the overall effect was an invasion of vertiginous ears that could no longer tell where the sounds and voices were coming from and whether they were outside or inside the listener's head. "The explosion of acoustic media flips over into an implosion which crashes with headlong immediacy into the very centre of perception." (1982: 472). The brain has become one with all that arrives from the outside. In *Gramophone, Film, Typewriter* the same analysis is applied to David Gilmour's "Fat Old Sun" from *Atom Heart Mother* which contains the command "And if you sit don't make a sound / Pick your feet up off the ground." In other words, the listener is ordered to assume a certain silent position when putting on a record to listen to "a silver sound."

> And what transpires then is indeed a strange and unheard-of silver noise. Nobody knows who is singing – the voice called David Gilmour that sings the song, the voice referred to by the song, or maybe the voice of the listener who makes no sound and is nonetheless supposed to sing once all the conditions of magic have been met. An unimaginable closeness of sound technology and self-awareness, a simulacrum of a feedback loop relaying sender and receiver. A song sings to a listening ear, telling it to sing. As if the music were originating in the brain itself, rather than emanating from stereo speakers or headphones. (Kittler 1999: 36–7)

According to Derrida, the fact that we can hear ourselves speak (or, as Kittler would add, sing) was the anchoring point for a long-lasting metaphysics of presence. But under new media-technological conditions, the philosophically portentous inner voice that Goethe's poem could merely conjure up in the symbolic register of words can now be technologically simulated inside our skull. Unlike the voices coming from singers on stage, these voices "implode in our ears [. . .] As if there were no distance between the recorded voice and listening ears, as if voices traveled along the transmitting bones of self-perception directly from the mouth into the ear's labyrinth, hallucinations become real" (Kittler 1999: 37). In older words, songs may have been about love and death; now they are about self-implosion: "'Brain Damage' doesn't sing of love or other such themes; it is one single feedback between sound and listeners' ears. Sounds proclaim what sounds have wrought and what surpasses all the effects Old Europe hoped to gain from the Book of Books or immortal poets" (1982: 475).

So what, then, is the brain damage the song announces in its title? It quite simply means, to quote the lyrics, that "there's someone in my head but it's not me." Here three levels of analysis intersect. The first is the conventional interpretation that rehashes traditional Pink Floyd lore, according to which "Brain Damage" (much like "Shine On You Crazy Diamond") is a paean to Syd Barrett. In an uneasy mixture of regret and relief, the song invokes Barrett's departure from Pink Floyd and his exile to a "diagnostic no-man's-land between LSD-psychosis and schizophrenia" (1982: 469), otherwise known as *The Dark Side of the Moon*. But, in Kittler's reading, "Brain Damage" also alludes to a possible return of – or rather *to* – the excluded, for the song may well induce its own title, in which case the band will truly start playing "different tunes" and thus join their former leader on the dark side of the moon, that is, in madness. Using the most up-to-date recording technology, "Brain Damage," then, performs the age-old association of moons with madness.

The second level – one clearly indebted to Deleuzian and early Foucauldian strands of French poststructuralism – is built around the question: what is madness? Or rather: what sounds mad in the age of reason? Answer: madness is the compulsive, incessant talking about the rules, protocols, and institutions that make us talk; it is, in Kittler's words, the unstoppable "discourse on discourse channel conditions" (Kittler, 1982: 473) – a diagnosis that looks more impressive when compressed into a German compound noun: *ein Diskurs über Diskurskanalbedingungen*. Obviously, branding this as madness presupposes that sane discourses are perceived to be individual speech acts presided over by an autonomous subject. Sanity means being in control of what you say; madness is the compulsion to incessantly talk about that which makes you talk. The "loonies" (as well as the engineers) are well aware of this: "Lunatics appear to be more informed than their doctors. They spell out that madness, rather than babbling metaphorically of radio transmitters in one's brain, is, quite on the contrary, a metaphor of technologies" (Kittler 1982: 472f.). The cliché that comes to mind is the crazy vagrant on the subway, babbling about the remote control devices the CIA implanted in his brain.

This points to the third, truly Kittlerian level: "Brain Damage" performs itself. It is a complex recording that technologically simulates its own title to such a degree that madness and music are as difficult to tell apart as outside and inside voices. Unlike Goethe's "Wanderer's Nightsong," however, which could only refer to intruding voices by way of writing, "Brain Damage" manipulates sound, thus performing the media-technological structures that make us what we are by making us speak. "Wanderer's Nightsong" is a poem that proclaims and performs what poetry can do, while conjuring up how poetry's effects came about. "Brain Damage" is a song that sings of the conditions under which it is sung, by providing its own technologically simulated genealogy. And that, of course, is the difference: Goethe is stuck with words; Pink Floyd operates in the realm of media technology.

2. SKULLS WITHOUT SPIRIT: MEDIA TECHNOLOGIES OF THE DISCOURSE NETWORK 1900

Kittler started to fully focus on media in the early 1980s. In hindsight, the shift from discourse analysis to *Medienwissenschaft* ("media studies," though the more literal translation would be "media science") seems both logical and inevitable. The desire to provide a concrete historical footing for Foucault's epistemic regimes and Lacan's psychic inscription practices had led Kittler into a detailed assessment of the materialities of communication that characterized the late eighteenth and early nineteenth centuries. Moving forward in time to the late nineteenth and early twentieth centuries required a similar focus on the new analog recording and storage technologies that challenged the alpha status of scriptographic production and typographic reproduction techniques of the Gutenberg Galaxy. But it was not only a matter of progressing from the Gutenbergian writing practices of the Discourse Network 1800 to the Edisonian media of the Discourse Network 1900; it was also a matter of recognizing the basic fact that the former, too, were and always had been media technologies. And this, Kittler argues, is something Foucault failed to realize. Hunting down documents in libraries in Paris, Warsaw, or Uppsala, Foucault "simply forgot" that "[e]ven writing itself, before it ends up in libraries, is a communication medium" (Kittler 1999:

5). Throughout his career Foucault remained a thinker of archives and libraries rather than of technologies; for all his admirable inspections of discursive regimes and effects, he shied away from analyzing what happens when the processing of discourse networks is entrusted to modern storage and recording devices. "It is for this reason that all his analyses end up immediately before that point in time at which other media penetrated the library's stacks. Discourse analysis cannot be applied to sound archives or towers of film rolls" (Kittler 1999: 5). In short, Kittler technologizes and extends Foucault. He plays Marx to Foucault's Hegel by turning discourse analysis onto its media-technological feet.

But, as the comparison between Goethe's "Wanderer's Nightsong" and Pink Floyd's "Brain Damage" has already made clear, writing may be a "communication medium" but it does not operate like a camera or a phonograph. In order to emphasize this distinction Kittler, regardless of a certain tautological ring, frequently refers to the latter as "technological media" (*technische Medien*). What is the pivotal difference? Writing operates by way of a symbolic grid which requires that all data "pass through the bottleneck of the signifier" (1999: 4), whereas phono-, photo- and cinematagraphic analog media process physical effects of the real. The trees and birds of Goethe's poem are word-signs that stand at a considerable remove from the real things, but the photo of a tree or the recording of birdsong presuppose – at least in pre-digital times – that at one point trees and birds were around. The data obtained and processed are the result of storing light and sound waves reflecting off, or emanating from, trees and birds. In this context Kittler likes to quote the film theorist Rudolf Arnheim, who said of medial reproductions that "[t]hey are not only supposed to resemble the object but rather guarantee this resemblance by being, as it were, a product of the object in question, that is, by being mechanically produced by it" (Arnheim, quoted in Kittler 1999: 11–12). Arts give way to media; aesthetic styles are replaced by technical standards. This is such an obvious and straightforward distinction that even Germanists in the 1980s understood it. Problems and controversies arose because of the implications: if the eighteenth-century materialities of communication had indeed been so instrumentally involved in the construction of high-profile cultural entities such as souls, subjects, and states, then the replacement of the hermeneutically glamorized writing technologies of the Discourse Network 1800 by the analog media of the Discourse Network 1900 could not but affect culture at its most basic level. What happens to souls in the age of Edison? This is a long and at times convoluted narrative that takes up the second part of *Discourse Networks* and all of the more accessible *Gramophone, Film, Typewriter*, a book Kittler himself describes as "*Discourse Networks* for kids" (Kittler and Weinberger 2009: 100). In order to get a grip on its implications, it is best to select, separate, and simplify the key components of the media shift.

Kittler ties the development of nineteenth-century analog media and related technological innovations to simultaneous advances in the analysis of human cognition and perception. The exact nature of the relationship between psychophysical research and media-technological progress is not quite clear; it appears to be a kind of feedback in the course of which cerebral and technical data-processing operations are constantly modeled on each other. As Kittler would have it, the shift emerges around the mid-nineteenth century; and it begins, as we would expect in a Kittlerian context, with war and destruction:

> Nature, the most pitiless experimenter, paralyzes certain
> parts of the brain through strokes and bullet wounds to the

head; research (since the Battle of Solferino in 1859) is only
required to measure the resulting interferences in order to
distinguish the distinct subroutines of in anatomically precise ways. Sensory aphasia (while hearing), dyslexia (while
reading), expressive aphasia (while speaking), agraphia
(while writing) bring forth machines in the brain. (1999:
189).

How "nature" can be credited with "bullet wounds" is probably even beyond Kittler's powers of explanation, but the
basic argument is clear: handicaps and crippled brains isolate
and highlight cognitive subroutines. Methodologically, this
is not an original idea; it was first given a scientific foundation by the French physiologist Claude Bernard (1813–1878)
who – not coincidentally – was of importance to Marshall
McLuhan. As the founder of experimental medicine, Bernard
advocated the diagnostic benefits of exploratory vivisection:
remove a liver or a spleen, observe and measure the resulting physiological changes, and you will be able to pinpoint
the function of the extracted organ. For Kittler, this practice
of determining function by way of malfunction also applies
to cognitive operations: "Blindness and deafness, precisely
when they affect either speech or writing, yield what would
otherwise be beyond reach: information on the human information machine" (1999: 189). In cool Kittlerese: "Cripples
and handicaps lie like corpses along the technical path to the
present" (2010: 120).

The difference is that livers, spleens, and kidneys were
seen as separate organs, whereas speaking, writing, hearing, or reading were traditionally subsumed under grandiose
headings such as *Geist* or *Bewusstsein* (spirit or consciousness). Here, Kittler's focus on discontinuity once again rears
its head. As described in the preceding chapter, one of the
fundamental psychic techniques of the Discourse Network

1800 was the smooth, effortless transition of graphemes into acoustic and visual signs, and vice versa. It was this systematic blurring of the boundaries between speaking, listening, reading, and writing that enabled the construction of language as a homogenous alpha-medium, able to weave together nature and culture in a continuum of meaning that subsequently was explored and exploited by writers and philosophers. The net outcome of this fusion of data-processing techniques was a subject fully in command of language, because it appeared to be so fully in command of the various ways in which language was produced, recorded, and communicated that everything seamlessly blended into each other. Precisely this continuity is destroyed by the media-technological shift commonly associated with pioneers and tinkerers like Bell and Edison. The essence of this shift was a *technological differentiation of data streams* and the subsequent ability *to store and manipulate real-time data*. The new photo- and phonographic media provided optical and acoustic data with their own storage and communication channels that no longer depended on symbolic mediation. Sights and sounds that hitherto had to be conjured up in the trained mind of the alphabetized reader were now presented directly to eyes and ears. And, with the advent of the typewriter, writing itself was mechanized – a mechanization that removed hands from writing surfaces and replaced the continuous flow of ink on paper (so important to Hegel and Lindhorst) with discrete, typographically standardized letters.

The implications are enormous. Take, for instance, the inevitable demotion of literature. The status it enjoyed in the Discourse Network 1800 rested on the fact that it actively performed, maintained, and recycled the fundamental hermeneutic features attributed to language. It is no surprise that Hoffmann's "Golden Pot" – the tell-all tale of the Discourse Network 1800 – is full of alchemical refer-

ences and narrative, for reading had become an alchemy
of the mind: it converted (as in the case of the inspired
Anselmus) lead letters into imaginary gold, symbols into
sights and sounds. To read was to raise and cultivate a soul,
to internalize the fundamental order of culture and nature,
and to extend an empire of meaning across the expanse of
being. To read was to exorcize meaningless noise in favor
of omnipresent meaning. All this changed with the arrival of
the new analog media. Inevitably, Kittler argues, literature
was debunked and lost its cultural importance. Why simulate
acoustic and optical data with words if they can be directly
recorded, stored, and transmitted without any recourse to
symbolic mediation? Why bother with the awkward relationship of language to time if new technologies are able
to store and manipulate real-time data flows? In Hamlet's
words, phonographic and photographic storage devices made
it abundantly clear that every text under the sun is nothing
but "words, words, words." Under these inauspicious intermedial conditions writers are left with two options: they can
either withdraw into the esoteric realm of (post)modernist
prose or subserviently mimic the new technologies. In other
words, they can either be James Joyce or Michael Crichton;
they can either produce *Finnegan's Wake*, the self-reflexive,
self-enclosed unfilmable work of word art, or *Jurassic Park*,
the text that aspires to be a film script. The fate of literature
in the age of mechanical and digital reproduction, then, is
either intramedial autism or intermedial serfdom.

This diagnosis, no doubt, is as crass as it is crude. Kittler
is neither interested in the ways in which the nineteenth-
century novel attempted to co-opt the achievements of the
bourgeoning technological media, nor does he consider the
flexible ways in which twentieth-century narrative prose
engages with analog and digital technologies (for a detailed
analysis see Wutz 2009). The justified criticism of Kittler's

reductionist take on modern literature, however, tends to miss out on a crucial point – a point that draws into question the standard label of Kittler as a "poststructuralist" media theoretician. If the impact of analog media is related to the fact that they can store and communicate the acoustic and optical data, which hitherto were only symbolically encoded in writing, does this not imply some kind of connection between the former and the latter? But if there is some kind of connection, is the media shift really one of those decisive ruptures that preclude all talk of continuity? "The history of every art form," Walter Benjamin famously noted in *The Work of Art in the Age of Mechanical Reproduction*, "shows critical epochs in which a certain art form aspires to effects which could be fully obtained only with a changed technical standard" (Benjamin 1969: 237). Exactly: the reading practices of the Discourse Network 1800 created a demand for media experiences that could only be met by post-print technologies. The hermeneutic cultivation of reading prepared the grounds for its supersession.

Here we can observe Kittler gradually distancing himself from the apodictic pronouncements of his first incarnation as a "poststructuralist" theorist. On the one hand, his move into media studies served to corroborate his programmatic as well as polemical emphasis on ruptures. Foucault spoke of epistemes that changed without rhyme or reason; Kittler was able to ascertain that these changes were related to media shifts (or at least to changing medial practices). Gramophone, film, and typewriter put an end to the Discourse Network 1800 and ushered in the Discourse Network 1900. There were no analog media in the age of Goethe (and if there had been it would have been a very different age), hence there can be no Goethes in the age of analog media. On the other hand, Kittler is much too good a historian to seriously believe in immaculate media conception. New media do not drop unannounced out of the sky like meteoroids or extraterrestrial Transformers. But given his strong anti-sociological, anti-economist, and anti-humanist bias against grounding technological innovations in social context, economic imperatives, or the desires of individual or collective subjects, the only explanation left is to posit an autonomous media-technological evolution driven by an internal dynamic. Of Gutenberg's letterpress, Kittler writes that it "made the techniques that supersede it – from photography to the computer – possible in the first place. It was the unique medium that set other media free" (2010: 67). Media react to media; "they follow each other in a rhythm of escalating strategic answers" (1997: 121). Humans are at best along for the ride; more precisely, they are the nodes and operators necessary to keep the process going until the time arrives at which media are able to interact and evolve without any human go-between. That, however, smacks far less of technologized Foucault than of an updated Hegel; it is a hidden grand narrative to which we shall return later on.

But back to cultural fabrications that were eroded in the Discourse Network 1900: literature may be important but it pales in significance to the question of language. What happens to language under new media-technological conditions? And given the complicity of subservient language and masterful subject in the Discourse Network 1800, how does the changing status of language change "so-called man"? Here, we enter one of the most brilliant and thought-provoking portions of Kittler's analysis. Once again, a literary text will serve as a helpful backdoor entrance, one that is as helpful in understanding the Discourse Network 1900 as "The Golden Pot" was for the Discourse Network 1800. Unfortunately, it is so well known that few care to read it closely any more: Bram Stoker's *Dracula*.

3. DRACULA'S PHONOGRAPH MEETS
ZARATHUSTRA'S TYPEWRITER

Readers know the story. Count Dracula, depicted by Stoker as a medieval potentate from the backwoods of Eastern Europe, is planning to turn Britain into his undead fiefdom. In order to prepare this "reverse colonization" (Arata 1990), Dracula learns English, studies Karl Marx's favorite reading material, the Victorian Red and Blue books, and retains the services of Jonathan Harker, an unfortunate real estate agent dispatched to Transylvania. Eager to recruit disposable minions even before he sets foot and claw on English soil, Dracula starts to exert a kind of telepathic remote control over a man called Renfield, who promptly ends up in a mental institution raving about the impending arrival of the "master." In lay terms, Renfield is mad. But what is madness? Or, to rephrase that more cautiously: what sounds mad in the age of reason? It is the apparent inability to control one's speech, especially if that very lack of control is central to what you are trying to say. Madness, in other words, is the most revealing form of the "discourse on discourse channel conditions" (Kittler 1982: 473). Obviously, branding this as madness presupposes that "discourses are perceived as individual speech acts" (ibid.), presided over by an autonomous subject that is not a mere talking machine or a ventriloquist's dummy attached to discursive or media-technological structures. It will, therefore, take a lot to diagnose and control the source of Renfield's lack of control.

The supervising doctor is Jack Seward, and his diagnostic practice is of particular interest to Kittler's repeated readings of Stoker's novel (see Kittler 1997: 50–84; 1999: 86–7). Seward realizes that he cannot grasp his patient's madness by straightforward rational analysis. Rather, his own thought processes – more precisely, the subconscious processes that have not yet emerged into consciousness – will have to match Renfield's. Somehow, Renfield's subconscious will have to be transferred and mapped onto Seward's, following which Seward will study his own subconscious processes in order to reveal what is troubling Renfield. "There is a method in his [Renfield's] madness, and the rudimentary idea in my mind is growing. It will be a whole idea soon, and then, oh, unconscious cerebration! You will have to give the wall to your conscious brother!" (Stoker 1975: 71). This may sound like an impossible task, but Doctor Seward has the right tool at his disposal: a phonograph. There are, in fact, a lot of phonographs in *Dracula*, which is strange because Britain never warmed to them, due to the exorbitant prices charged by the Edison-Bell Company (Gelatt 1977: 101). Seward listens to his patient, then he rushes to his phonograph and records his uncensored associations which, once they are transcribed and open to conscious and deliberate inspection, will reveal what is behind Renfield's rambling. Ultimately there are two phonographs involved: the real one which Seward uses to record his own associations, and Seward's unconscious which apparently can record Renfield's unconscious with the indiscriminate receptiveness of Edison's new recording device.

Kittler's reading of this technologically facilitated double logorrhea is as straightforward as it is ingenious: Seward is practicing what Freud, following the suggestion of one of his patients, had called a talking cure, but it is a talking cure that *literally enacts what Freud had only referred to metaphorically.* Freud stated that the analyst must open his own mind to the uncensored talk of the patient in order to establish a direct communion – if not some kind of communion – between his own unconscious and that of the patient.

To put it in a formula, he [the doctor/GWY] must turn his own unconscious like a receptive organ towards the transmitting unconsciousness of the patient. He must adjust himself to the patient as a telephone receiver is adjusted to the transmitting microphone. Just as the receiver converts back into sound waves the electric oscillations in the telephone line which were set up by sound waves, so the doctor's unconscious is able, from the derivatives of the unconsciousness which are communicated to him, to reconstruct that unconscious, which has determined the patient's free associations. (Freud XII, 1962: 115–16)

Kittler reads passages like this much as Freud himself listened to his patients. Just as the analyst, in order to reveal what the patient is repressing, privileges unintentional and sublexical clues over intended utterances, Kittler takes literally what Freud introduced as mere metaphors and comparisons. Psychoanalysis is not *like* phonography or telephony, it *is* phonography, because it accepts and enacts the new ways humans are determined by the technical standards of the Discourse Network 1900:

> Freud's materialism reasoned only so far as the information machines of his era – no more, no less. Rather than continuing the dream of the Sprit as origin, he described a "psychic apparatus" (Freud's wonderful word choice) that implemented all available transmission and storage media. (Kittler 1997: 134)

Psychoanalysis has a phonographic a priori. The crux of Freud's (and Seward's) talking cure is that "so-called Man" is not in command of language. Language is a data stream that can be recorded; moreover, it is precisely the fact that it can be recorded, transcribed, and scrutinized that reveals it to be a data stream operating according to its own rules. Sooner or later it will betray rather than constantly obey the conscious ego of the speaker. The introduction of impassive mechanical sound-recording technologies, then, constitutes the main enabling factor for a fundamental reassessment of language, at the core of which is a reversal of the traditional relationship between speaker and language. We do not speak; we are spoken. We are all remote-controlled Renfields; we are the singer of "Brain Damage" who can no longer distinguish between inside and outside voices. As already alluded to in the analysis of the Pink Floyd teaser at the outset of this chapter, the Discourse Network 1900 reveals madness – the inability to produce discourse as individual speech acts – to be the true state of affairs. "Lunatics appear to be more informed than their doctors. They spell out that madness is [. . .] a metaphor of technologies" (Kittler 1982: 472f.). In the famous words of Arthur C. Clarke, any sufficiently advanced technology is indistinguishable from magic; for Kittler, any sufficiently advanced media technology is indistinguishable from madness – at least, as long as we believe that being in command of our speech acts is the hallmark of reason.

Doctor Seward never lives up to the potential of his gadgets. He fails to grasp what Renfield is talking about, and he is unable to save the woman he loves, Lucy Westenra, from becoming Dracula's first and only English middle-class victim. It takes more than garlic and talking cures to defeat the vampire; ultimately, he is overcome by a fully mobilized media link-up, involving several phonographs, a Kodak camera, one of the very first cameo performances by a telephone in modern literature, excessive use of the British postal services, a couple of messenger boys, and a transcontinental telegraph system originating in the Crimean War (see Winthrop-Young 1994). Stoker's novel truly is the "heroic epic of the final victory of technological media over the blood-sucking despots of old Europe" (Kittler 1999: 86). Dracula is aware of the danger he is in and at one point destroys all the manuscripts and Seward's phonograph cylinders, but he does not realize that there are copies in a safe. The undead stand no chance against the powers of mechanical reproduction.

But the most important gadget is Mina Harker's typewriter. Faithfully transcribing diaries, letters, logbooks, and phonograph roll, it is instrumental in exposing Dracula's plans, movements, and hiding places. For Kittler, the use of Mina's secretarial skills is the most interesting feature of Stoker's novel next to Seward's phonographic talking cure. Mina is a former assistant schoolmistress who has learned shorthand and typewriting, yet she refuses to translate her marketable media expertise into social advancement as a "new woman." On the contrary, she starts out as a woman caught in the Discourse Network 1800, happy to inspire and receive Transylvanian letters from her future husband Jonathan. But the urgent need to mobilize the data-processing facilities necessary to defeat Dracula, whose planned hostile takeover can be read as a depiction of the nineteenth-control control crisis that could only be overcome by the acceleration and integration of informational goods (Winthrop-Young 1994), calls for Mina's skills and she turns into "the central relay station of an immense information network" (Kittler 1990: 354). Mina's career embodies the fate of women in the Discourse Network 1900. The sexually closed circuits of the Discourse Network 1800 are breached; women who hitherto had been confined to the input and output position as muses and readers, respectively, become an integral part of discourse production. They now perform on a professional level what Mina had wanted to do exclusively for Jonathan in the privacy of their home, "to take down what he wants to say [. . .] and write it out for him on the typewriter" (Stoker 1975: 58).

If, in Wellbery's concise summary, the Discourse Network

1800 revolved around "the discursive production of the Mother as the source of discursive production" (1990: xxiii), then the removal of Mother/Woman/Nature puts an end to the guarantee of meaningfulness explored and exploited by poets and philosophers. If language no longer originates from the Mother's Mouth, all the noise that reaches the ear of Goethe's wanderer – chirping, twittering, blowing, and swaying – is just that and nothing more: *noise*. Language is no longer a homogenous transparent medium; and whatever messages it may contain are no longer grounded in the always already meaningful constituent components (the "minimal signifieds"), but are the effect of statistically computable arrangements of meaningless elements. Women are no longer mothers and makers of meaning, but at best recorders and arrangers of temporarily meaningful noise.

How does the typewriter play into this? More than any other nineteenth-century technological innovation, it embodies the two closely related key features of the Discourse Network 1900, *separation and discontinuity*, which not coincidentally happen to be the opposite of the key features of the Discourse Network 1800, transition and continuity. As discussed in the context of the writing lessons in Hoffmann's "Golden Pot", the production of the indivisible subject self was linked to continuous handwriting. Now the flow of ink and the direct connection between hand, pen, and paper is replaced by standardized, discreet letter signs mechanically produced by a contraption that separates the hand from script. Heidegger was one of the first philosophers to be deeply concerned by this. Playing on the strong connection in German between *Hand* (hand) and *handeln* ("to act"; still present in English in the phrase "to handle matters"), which allowed him to present the hand as "the essential distinction of man" because "[m]an himself acts [*handelt*] through the hand [*Hand*]," Heidegger concluded that "when writing was withdrawn from the origin of its essence, i.e., from the hand, and was transferred to the machine, a transformation occurred in the relation of Being to man" (Heidegger 1992: 80). The notion that the introduction of a data-processing technology is, to use Heidegger's term, a rupture in the very "history of being" (*Seinsgeschichte*), will return with a vengeance in the next, Greek, chapter. Suffice it to say that Heidegger's baffling digression on the typewriter must be seen against the background of the long-standing philosophical embellishment of handwriting.

Heidegger, however, was not the first philosopher to reflect on typewriters. That honor belongs to Nietzsche, the first philosopher to actually use a typewriter. Plagued by myopia, Nietzsche had ordered a Danish Malling Hansen "writing ball," a spiky contraption that looked like a Cubist hedgehog, and for the very short time in which the machine was in working condition he managed to type a few letters and poems. In response to an inquiry from a friend whether the machine had an effect on his style, Nietzsche responded with a statement that contains most of modern media theory from Innis and McLuhan onwards: *Unser Schreibzeug arbeitet mit an unseren Gedanken* – "Our writing tools are also working on our thoughts" (Nietzsche, quoted in Kittler 1999: 200). In an extensive reading, Kittler tries to show how the mechanics of the typewriter reappear in Nietzsche's genealogical analysis, according to which humans are not blessed with inborn faculties such as knowledge, speech, and virtue, but are in fact no more than walking, talking memory machines. Crouched over his mechanically defective writing ball, the physiologically defective philosopher came to realize that humans have changed their position "from the agency of writing to an inscription surface" (Kittler 1999: 210). But ultimately it is Nietzsche's fate rather than his thought that becomes paradigmatic for the Discourse Network 1900.

Kittler started *Discourse Networks* with a reading of the most famous reading scene in German literature. Goethe's Faust appears on stage to perform a translation exercise that would have him kicked out of any ancient Greek beginners' class: John 1:1, "In the beginning was the *Word*," is twisted into "In the beginning was the *Act*." This is not translation; this is hermeneutics – an imperial, self-aggrandizing hermeneutic hubris that subjects all of creation to a regime of meaning, turning the world into a semantic playground for the inspired male subject. At the other end there is Nietzsche – not the Nietzsche of popular renown with the fearful pronouncements on women, Christianity, and morals, and the even more intimidating moustache, but the tragic spectacle of the insane Nietzsche in the last years of his life, "screaming inarticulately," mindlessly filling notebooks with simple "writing exercises," and "happy in his element as long as he had pencils" (Kittler 1990: 182). This is the ground zero of hermeneutics at the center of the Discourse Network 1900: no spirit, no soul, no guaranteed meaning, but only a body in all its vulnerable nakedness, media technologies in all their mindless impartiality, and between them an exchange of noise that only focused delusion can arrange into deeper meaning.

4. WRITE TEXT TO POWER: *PROGRAMMARE AUDE!*

In the course of the 1980s Kittler turned his attention toward digital technology. His concern was as theoretical as it was practical, for unlike the majority of media theorists who crossed over from literature or sociology into media studies, Kittler spent years gathering hands-on experience. While many object to his more outlandish views, few deny that he knows what he is talking about. If Nietzsche was the first renegade philologist to use a typewriter, Kittler is the first renegade Germanist to teach computer programming. The result is, once again, a stimulating mix of expertise and extremism. All the important and contested points appear early on, in this quote from the introduction to *Gramophone, Film, Typewriter*:

> The general digitization of channels and information erases the difference among individual media. Sound and image, voice and text are reduced to surface effects, known to consumers as interface. Sense and the senses turn into eyewash. Their media-produced glamour will survive for an interim as a by-product of strategic programs. Inside the computers themselves everything becomes a number, quantity without image, sound, or voice. And once optical fiber networks turn formerly distinct data flows into a standardized series of digitized numbers, any medium can be translated into any other. With numbers, nothing is impossible. Modulation, transformation, synchronization; delay, storage, transposition; scrambling, scanning, mapping – a total media link on a digital basis will erase the very concept of medium. Instead of wiring people and technologies, absolute knowledge will run as an endless loop. (1999: 1–2; translation amended)

Let us take a look at some of the points raised here. Digital technology comes with a certain messianic finality: once it has arrived there will be nothing else, no further history, at least no further history of technology, to speak of. Since this pronouncement Kittler has softened his stance and wondered about the possibility of future analog or quantum computers (see Gane and Sale 2007), but whatever not-Von-Neumann design may arise in the future, it will not change the erasure "of the very concept of medium." Note that

Kittler is talking about concepts rather than about media as such. Media continue to exist but they have suffered a demotion. Much like impoverished aristocrats who now work as tourist guides on their former estates, media are no longer located at the crucial intersection of physical processes and the human sensory apparatus; they have been moved to the margin of the digital machine in order to allow humans some access to this self-contained numerical universe:

> There are physiological-physical computer interfaces that can still be regarded as media. But on the inside, in the hardware or software, there's nothing imaginary. In this sense: Facing laymen and people, media are the visible sides of a world that science invokes as the *dark side of the moon*. (Kittler and Weinberger 2009: 101)

Media are the computer's concession to our inferiority; their existence is due to the inability of any living being – with the exception of Neo, the hero of the *Matrix* trilogy – to directly interface with digital processing on the inside.

But what irks Kittler is that, despite all this, user-friendly *software* tricks us into believing that we are in charge of the computer. We continue to think of computers as mere tools, and this, in turn, serves to perpetuate our narcissistic self-image as *homo faber*, man the toolmaker. All the polemical energy once reserved for the glorification of the enlightened subject is redirected toward software. No other media theorist has attacked it with such passion; indeed, so bent is Kittler on exposing the hollowness of software that he came to deny its very existence. There is no software because it can be reduced to basic hardware operations:

> Not only no program, but also no underlying microprocessor system could ever start without the rather incredible

autobooting faculty of some elementary functions that, for safety's sake, are burnt into silicon and thus form part of the hardware [. . .] Any transformation from entropy into information, from a million sleeping transistors into differences between electronic potentials, necessarily presupposes a material even called reset. [. . .] All code operations [. . .] come down to absolutely local string manipulations, that is, I am afraid, *to signifiers of voltage differences*. (Kittler 1997: 150; emphasis in the original)

The Discourse Network 1900 discovered a skull without spirit; it is now a matter of discovering the spiritless mainframe. Kittler is debunking software in much the same way as nineteenth-century science pried apart the human mind by examining how the brain works. Ultimately, there is no software for the same reason that there is no higher faculty known as *Geist*, mind or spirit: both are no more than fleeting configurations that can be reduced to the switching on and off of countless tiny circuits routed through hollow containers made of tin, bone, or plastic.

But, much to Kittler's chagrin, the fact that this "postmodern Tower of Babel" is at base a hardware configuration has been "explicitly contrived to evade our perception" (1997: 148). This is where the argument moves from technological reductionism to a technologically evolved version of ideology criticism. Operating systems, especially those with names like "Windows," promise unobstructed transparency, but are in fact one-way mirrors. Like invisible police investigators examining a suspect, the computer sees us; looking at the computer, we only see ourselves. We are, quite literally, screened off from our computers, and precisely this allows us to be full of ourselves. User-friendly machines that conceal their non-human internal operations allow humans to conceal from themselves that their self-descriptions are the deposit of equally non-human discursive processes. "[T]hrough the use of keywords like user-interface, user-friendliness or even data projection, the industry has damned humanity to remain human" (1997: 157).

Ironically, this software criticism echoes some of the rhetoric of the social movements that Kittler avoided in his student days. Software is condemned as the new opium for the people; it is dispensed by forces that are bent on keeping the untrusted user masses from taking over the digital means of production. Hence we should discard those fancy operating systems and resort to the text-based teletype interface that prevailed in the early days of computing, or join the LINUX bandwagon. We must study basic programming and operating languages in order to overcome their dependence on the software opium handed out by the industry. In his famous pamphlet *What Is Enlightenment?*, Immanuel Kant had chided the "self-caused immaturity" that keeps us from using our mental faculties without the guidance of another: "The motto of enlightenment is therefore *Sapere Aude!* Have courage to use your own intelligence!" (Kant 1949: 132). With all the activist concern and fervor he normally shies away from, Kittler intones a similar rallying cry: *Programmare Aude!* Have courage to use your own programming skills! And while this results neither in Western Enlightenment nor in any mastery over digital machines, it will at least enable us to rise above our self-caused software-supported immaturity and interact eye to eye (or signal to signal) with all that is on the verge of leaving us behind. In an ironic and highly quotable exaggeration, the media theorist Frank Hartmann, one of Kittler's most astute and incisive critics, claimed that what Kittler ultimately has in mind is a "machine whisperer," somebody who – like a character from Neal Stephenson's *Snow Crash* – has such mastery over the machine code that he can directly interact with basic operating levels of digital systems without any need for intermediary software programs. The precondition would be the fulfillment of the grand dreams of Leibniz and Turing: the complete conversion of thinking into computation (see Hartmann 1998).

To retrieve the concluding remarks of the preceding chapter, Kittler's iconoclast rhetoric, his disdain for fancy icons and narcosis-inducing software, is one of the last rallying cries emanating from that venerable and highly influential cultural institution, the German parsonage. Kittler – in his own words, the offspring of a "Lutheran family" (Kittler and Maresch 1994: 103) – appears to be advocating a computer-age *sola scriptura*, a digital Lutheranism in which Microsoft takes the place of the Vatican. A good Christian needs no clerical infrastructure to achieve a connection to God; a good user needs no fancy software interface to connect to cyberspace. (This anti-Catholic, or more specifically anti-Jesuit, stance is also noticeable in the historical accounts of the Counter-Reformation media tactics in *Optical Media*.) According to Nietzsche, the Protestant pastor was the "grandfather of German philosophy" (Nietzsche 2002: 28); and that makes him one of the great-grandfathers of German media theory.

5. ON THE SILICON BEACH: THE ENDS OF MAN AND MEDIA

But whether or not software exists, whether or not we remain immature human pods ensnared by Microsoft or escape into the free frontiers of text-based, open-source programming – those are minor matters. To return to the longer quote from *Gramophone Film Typewriter*, the main issue is a grand narrative whose vanishing point is nothing less than human obsolescence.

To repeat, what does digital technology do? All information is digitized, "which is why computers in principle comprehend all other media and can subject their data to the mathematical models of signal processing" (Kittler 1993: 187). The computer effectively de-differentiates the tripartite Edisonian Discourse Network 1900, which roughly a century earlier had technologically differentiated the homogenous alpha-medium language of the Discourse Network 1800. The result is a philosophically portentous 1-3-1 structure. A pristine unity (spiritualized language) is divided against itself and split up (analog differentiation in combination with the typewriter's mechanization), but this antithesis is in turn overcome by the unity of higher, i.e., digital, complexity. It is difficult not to think of this in pop-Hegelian terms: the Discourse Network 1900 is the antithesis to the Discourse Network 1800, and the digital Discourse Network 2000 (a term, incidentally, used far more often by Kittler's readers than by himself) sublates the two. Media theory points toward a veritable philosophy of media history.

A cryptic interview comment provides a first glimpse of what is at stake:

> What I keep dreaming of and what people don't like to hear because they believe that technology and science are mere tools made for people in the street [. . .] is that machines, especially the contemporary intelligent machines as conceived by [Alan] Turing in 1936, are not there for us humans – we are, as it were, built on too large a scale – , but that nature, this glowing, cognitive part of nature, is feeding itself back into itself [*sondern daß sich da die Natur, dieser leuchtende erkennende Teil der Natur, mit selbst selbst rückkoppelt*]. (Kittler 2003a: 270)

Hegel's philosophy presented history as the process through and by which the Absolute Spirit achieves self-understanding.

Evolving human consciousness is the stage on which the diremptions and syntheses are conceptualized, an ascending spiral heading toward the reconciliation of spirit and nature, be it in Hegel's beloved Prussia or elsewhere. Kittler is replacing Hegel's *Phenomenology of the Spirit* with – to borrow a title by the Austrian writer Robert Menasse – a "phenomenology of despiritualization." The ultimate subject of history is technology, understood in a very broad sense as the processing of nature that for an extended period of time was dependent on human intermediaries, but that now, with the arrival of digital technology, is closer to a self-processing of nature that leaves humans behind. The processing facilities of the human mind are no more than a transitory stage in an ever finer, ever more accelerated and complex feedback cycle that – in Lacan's terms – aims at establishing direct connections between the symbolic without any recourse to the imaginary. At one point in the long history of the encounter between media and bodies, there was a place and maybe a need for subjects; but once machines able to read and write without human input can take care of business on their own, such biological prostheses become obsolete. But Kittler is not simply rehashing the well-worn anthropocentric substitution story, according to which machine slaves programmed to simulate human thought processes will replace their human masters. He is not arguing that computers are artificial human brains, or that they digitally ape specifically human ways of thinking. Rather, they optimize certain patterns of information processing that were also imposed on human beings and that subsequently were mistaken for innately human qualities. Where subjects were, there programs shall be – because programs were there in the first place.

Which brings us back to the famous wager at the conclusion of *The Order of Things* that in consequence of some "outside event," the nature of which Foucault refuses to specify, "man would be erased, like a face drawn in sand at the edge of the sea." That outside event is the realm of media. By grounding Foucauldian discourse analysis in his own brand of media theory Kittler can be more specific: discursive regimes of the late eighteenth century drew the figure of man into the sand, and even if he manages to survive the etching, typing, and storing of the late nineteenth-century analog media, he is certain to disappear with the compression of that sand into silicon. The only thing that remains constant is the sound of the sea. That sound, incidentally, is referred to in German as *Rauschen*. A cognate of English "rustle," it also describes the swaying of trees and the rustling of hedges in the wind, and it is easily one of the most overused words in German poetry since the age of Goethe, primarily because of the way its onomatopoeic beauty conjures up natural sounds full of poetic significance. But in one of the most remarkable semantic extensions ever undertaken in any language, German physicists in the 1920s came to use *Rauschen* to denote a disturbance variable with a broad-frequency spectrum – what in English is called (white) *noise*. And this is maybe the shortest, most economic way to summarize the switch from the Discourse Network 1800 to 1900, and then on to the Discourse Network 2000 (a term Kittler hardly ever uses): from *Geist* to *Rauschen*, from philosophically promoted poetry and naturalized hermeneutics to stochastics and information theory, from the guarantee of an always already meaningful world to an environment of meaningless noise that can at best be momentarily arranged into allegedly significant patterns. And then, around the turn of the millennium, comes a sudden rupture in Kittler's oeuvre: the sea will still be there, but the air will be filled with very different sounds.

4

GREEK CULTURAL TECHNIQUES

1. THIRD TEASER: SIREN FACTS

deur' ag' iôn, poluain' Oduseu, mega kudos Achaiôn
(Homer 1996)

Or, in the language that some believe has the closest spiritual affinity to ancient Greek:

Los komm hierher, Odysseus vieler Rätsel, grosser Ruhm Achaias (Kittler 2006a: 51)

And in a more accessible insular dialect:

Come closer, famous Odysseus – Achaea's pride and
glory –
moor your ship on our coast so you can hear our song!
Never has any sailor passed our shores in his black
craft
until he has heard the honeyed voices pouring from
our lips,

and once he hears to his heart's content sails on, a
    wiser man.
We know all the pains that Achaeans and Trojans once
    endured
on the spreading plain of Troy when the gods willed it
    so –
all that comes to pass on the fertile earth, we know it
    all! (Homer 1996: 277)

This short passage from Book 12 of Homer's *Odyssey* is
known as the Song of the Sirens, a duo of singing temptresses who despite the brevity of their cameo performance
have enjoyed a remarkable philological and philosophical afterlife. They are also victims of remarkably bad press,
which is not surprising given that what little we learn about
them in the *Odyssey* comes straight from the mouth of antiquity's most accomplished liar.

Pietro Pucci has noted that many of the terms, epithets,
and phrases used by the Sirens do not occur elsewhere in the
Odyssey; they are instead much closer to the language of the
Iliad. The Sirens are addressing the post-Trojan vagabond of
the *Odyssey* as the intrepid Achaean mastermind of the *Iliad*,
and the seductiveness of their interpellation lies in its appeal
that the addressee reassume his former glory. By reproducing the diction of the older epic, Odysseus 2.0 is invited to
morph back into the original model and "to return to the
character of the *Iliad*" (Pucci 1998: 5). Odysseus resists, or,
rather, he ingeniously creates conditions that make it impossible for him to succumb to the temptation. This is not
the only time that echoes of the heroic exploits of the *Iliad*
intrude upon the *Odyssey* only to be repelled by grief or cunning. Listening to a stirring rendition of his own exploits at
Troy, Odysseus

> melted into tears,
> running down from his eyes to wet his cheeks
> as a woman weeps, her arms flung round her darling
>   husband,
> a man who fell in battle, fighting for town and
>   townsmen,
> trying to beat the day of doom from home and
>   children. (Homer 1996: 208)

The sacker of cities weeps like one of his victims. Countless readers have noted (some approvingly, others regretfully) that a sizeable ethical gap separates the two epics attributed to one and the same bard. As the post-heroic, domestically inclined *Odyssey* abandons the more martial *Iliad*, Odysseus leaves behind the two melodious temptresses whose song would lure him "out of the *Odyssey* to rot on their island" (Pucci 1998: 6).

Pucci's intertextual analysis revolves around the dangers of a seductive regression, which recalls the famous philosophical reading of the Siren episode in Horkheimer and Adorno's *Dialectic of Enlightenment*. If Pucci's Odysseus faces the danger of losing himself in a past text, the Odysseus of Horkheimer and Adorno is faced with the possibility of losing himself in the past itself. Succumbing to the Sirens is tantamount to regressing to an earlier, archaic state of existence that would undo the fragile form of individual selfhood Odysseus has built up through cunning and sacrifice. The voyage home to Ithaca "is the way taken through the myths by the self" (Horkheimer and Adorno 1972: 46) – a self that can only emerge by subjugating both inner and outer nature, and that remains as threatened by mythical forces as it is by the travails of climate and geography. Along the way the Sirens represent one of the most dangerous "powers of disintegration" (ibid.: 33); it is only by cunning, defined as "defiance in a rational form" (ibid.: 59), that Odysseus manages to withstand their allure. The "black ship" survives because it reproduces a class-based society: the proletarian crew, their ears stuffed with wax, keeps rowing on, while their lord, able to listen but unable to move, is tied to the mast. A potent combination of enforced self-denial with a suspiciously modern division of labor ensures that Odysseus – the *ur*-bourgeois who exposes himself to an aesthetic experience only under the condition that it will not truly affect him – will be able to listen to the Sirens without following their call.

Kittler's disdain for the "two popular hobby philosophers" (2006a: 263) Horkheimer and Adorno is palpable. He leaves no doubt that their reading of the Siren episode is as incompetent and amateurish as their influential analysis of media technology in the Culture Industry section of the *Dialectic of Enlightenment*. They know little about Homer; they do not care who or what (or where) the Sirens were; and they are utterly clueless when it comes to the complexity of the writing system that enabled, supported, and reproduced Homer's epic. It's all Greek to them – Greek being something they do not understand either. Kittler stages his reading of the Siren passage in direct competition with that of Horkheimer/Adorno. Once again, Freiburg – Heidegger's and Kittler's Freiburg, which is almost in earshot of Nietzsche's Basel – takes aim at Frankfurt, this time on Greek soil.

Kittler begins with a heady mix of gullibility and skepticism. He trusts Homer but is wary of Odysseus. Given the latter's notorious mendacity, why should we believe his account? He is so untrustworthy he even infects his sources. Circe – who as one of the many female deities bent on retaining the sexual services of Odysseus has a good motive for denouncing her competition – describes the Sirens as surrounded by "heaps of bone, / rotting away, rags of skin shriveling on their bones" (Homer 1996: 273). Not so, Kittler responds; if that were the case the stench alone would have kept all ships at a safe distance. Also, Odysseus's choice of words is suspect. Why does he use the plural form "*we could hear their song no more*" (Homer 1996: 277; emphasis added), if his security precautions ensured that he alone was able to hear the Sirens? And when describing how his ship "put that island astern" (ibid.), why does he use a verb that usually describes leaving rather than merely passing by? In addition there are, true to Kittler's heart, some very practical concerns. Following the old tradition that the Sirens frolicked on Li Galli, an archipelago of small islands located about 3 miles southwest of Positano off the Amalfi coast, and that Aeaea, the home of Circe, is Mount Circeo on Cape Circaeum, Odysseus and his crew would have covered 200 miles without interruption by the time they reached the Sirens. According to Circe, their island is full of flowery meadows, which indicates that it has fresh water. It is inconceivable, Kittler argues, that Odysseus would have traveled such a distance under a Mediterranean sun without replenishing his water supplies, especially with the long haul through the Straits of Messina watched over by Scylla and Charybdis still ahead of him. Odysseus is – once again – lying. He didn't sail past the singing duo, he landed on their island; and, given that he survived to tell the tale, the Sirens cannot be as murderous as Circe and countless yarns concocted later by inferior Roman scribblers make them out to be.

But if that isn't evidence enough, Kittler now delivers an empirical *coup de grâce* that concerns the song itself, or rather the fact that Odysseus is able to reproduce it verbatim. How close do you have to be to a source to understand it so perfectly? In April 2004 Kittler traveled to Amalfi and obtained a permit to visit the Li Galli islands, which are now a protected marine preserve. He placed two female singers on the beach and had himself rowed past. As anybody with any experience in outdoor acoustics could have predicted, he was able to *hear* the voices from quite a distance, but no matter how close the boat came to the shore (and it came within 10 meters), he could not *understand* them. The reason is simple: vowels carry far but consonants do not, and while the former "may impart the gift of music, consonants give that of language, the like of which Odysseus hears" (2006a: 58). In passing, Kittler also noted that the meadows mentioned by Circe are invisible from a boat; you have to step ashore to see them. Clearly, Odysseus left the boat. "Do not believe the greatest Greek liar," Kittler exhorts his readers, "but the two Sirens" (2006a: 58). In *Musen, Nymphen und Sirenen* (*Muses, Nymphs and Sirens*), an audio CD whose informal style of delivery offers a welcome antidote to the Heideggerian ruminations of *Musik und Mathematik*, Kittler provides a more straightforward assessment of his maritime exploit. "After 2,800 years we finally provided philology with an experimental footing rather than with textual masturbation (*Textwichserei*)" (Kittler 2005: 12 mins 20 secs–12mins 30 secs). *Quod erat demonstrandum.*

2. GREEK WRITING LESSONS

The Sirens? Homer? Ancient Greece? How did Kittler end up here? What does all this have to do with media technology or discursive practices, not to mention computers? Apart from drawing a considerable amount of skepticism from classicists, this large-scale reorientation – which in terms of ambition, scope, and sheer research tenacity resembles Harold Innis's turn to classical antiquity – has baffled and estranged even some of Kittler's most sympathetic observers. (Less compassionate voices would add that with advancing age Kittler and Innis share an inexorable descent into near-illegibility.) But, as in the case of Innis, there is more involved than cultural nostalgia or idiosyncratic research interests; ultimately, the excursion into antiquity is part of an attempt to provide a grand occidental narrative that centers on the basics of data processing and the feedback between the materialities of communication and changing world views. Or, to use the Heideggerian term that programs Kittler's Greek work, it is a matter of *Seinsgeschichte*, the history of being. We are, however, dealing with a work of progress that, should it ever be concluded, will encompass at least seven books, of which so far only two have been published. We can therefore only comment on a double beginning – the promising and baffling beginning of a major research project and the equally ambivalent beginning of occidental history.

The immediate connection to Kittler's prior media-historical work is the emergence of the Greek vowel alphabet. To briefly recapitulate commonly held views, around the eighth century BCE the Greeks are said to have adopted and adapted a Phoenician consonantal script. Some signs such as γ (*gamma*), δ (*delta*), and ε (*epsilon*) remained identical; others were either rotated around their axis (α), turned into their mirror image (λ), or raised into an upright position (Σ); and in the few remaining instances there is no clear logic to the change. In any case, *alpha beta gamma delta*, that most Greek of all sequences, is nothing but the Phoenician mnemonic device '*āleph bēth gīmel dāleth*. The most important modification was to have those letters designating consonants that did not exist in Greek refer to vowels instead. *Aleph*, which indicated a glottal stop, turned into *alpha* and came to stand for the vowel *a*, while Phoenician *he*, a voiceless glottal fricative, was refunctionalized into ε or *epsilon*, a close-mid front unrounded vowel. To be sure, the basic notion that vowels needed to be indicated in writing to avoid misunderstandings was not unique to ancient Greece. Several Semitic scripts featured so-called *matres lectionis* or "mothers of reading," that is, the use of consonants to indicate long vowels, but the Greek alphabet was the first to feature specific vowel signs. Leaving aside the difficult question of how many people were originally involved in this import venture, a lot of thought went into the adoption of the Phoenician script, but – and this is crucial for understanding Kittler's resolutely anti-philosophical take on Greek philosophy – a lot of thought came out if it too. We need to briefly summarize some of the most pertinent aspects in order to locate Kittler's position.

1. To fully appreciate what the Greek adapter(s) did, it is imperative to keep in mind that *identifying vowels serve to isolate consonants*. The latter no longer appear, as in so many syllabaries, always already attached to a vowel (*bee cee dee eff gee kay*), but as detached sound elements. However, while we keep encountering the former (we just need to voice any acronym from "ABC" to "ZZ Top"), we rarely come across pure consonants outside of elementary school classes or public readings of modernist language poetry. Like almost any other script, the Greek alphabet is not only a repository of signs but also an analysis of language; but, unlike almost all other scripts, it analyzes not what you hear but how you speak by cataloguing the basic building blocks of speech. The Greek adapter(s) – whoever he, she, or they may have been – most likely were not aware of this when they set out to modify the Phoenician script; if they had already analyzed their language to such an extent they would have devised their own alphabet. Rather, it was the encounter with an alien technique and the need to modify its sign system that revealed to the Greeks the fundamental constituent components of their own language. This is no doubt the historically most important instance of the rule that we invariably introspect language in terms laid down by our writing systems.

"Rather than viewing writing as an attempt to capture the existing knowledge of syntax, writing provided a model for speech, thereby making the language available for analysis into syntactic constituents, the primary one being words which then become the object of philosophical reflection as well as the object of definitions" (Olson 1994: 76). The fact that the adaptation of a sign system taught the Greeks how they themselves spoke corresponds directly to Kittler's assertion that "we know nothing about our senses until media provided models and metaphors" (2010: 34). Just as the nineteenth century discovered precisely those information machines in our brains that were being developed by Edison and others, the Greeks discovered the operations of speech in their encounter with an imported storage system.

2. There is a long-standing debate concerning the alleged superiority of the Greek vowel alphabet over its Eastern competitors, a debate that on occasion is fueled – deliberately or not – by Eurocentric, Orientalist, and even anti-Semitic presumptions. In a famous comparison between Utnapishtim's account of the great flood in the *Epic of Gilgamesh* and a description of flood fortifications in the twelfth book of the *Iliad*, the classicist Eric Havelock stressed the alleged superiority and greater mimetic facility of the vowel alphabet (Havelock 1978: 5–11). The Greek flood, simply put, is more fluent and fluid. Introducing a German translation of Havelock's writings, the Egyptologist Jan Assmann, whose work has had considerable influence on German debates on media and memory, took Havelock to task for what appears to be an insufficient appreciation of consonantal and hieroglyphic scripts: "We have to clearly emphasize that there is no sound, no word, no sentence, no thought of a given language that cannot be expressed in the writing system that belongs to it." (Assmann and Assmann 1990: 22). Kittler too tends to be slightly dismissive when discussing the stor-

age and recording capabilities of non-Greek scripts, such as Egyptian hieroglyphs. Given the older Kittler's more explicit emphasis on matters of love and rapture, his prime example comes as no surprise: "[N]obody knows how the heretic king Akhneten called his N-f-r-t-t when they were making children" (2006a: 105). Indeed we don't, which is why the English refer to her as *Nefertiti* while the Germans prefer *Nofretete*. Assmann would respond by pointing out that the Egyptians themselves knew and that they were fully capable of transcribing and subsequently vocalizing her name in ways that resembled Akhneten's connubial exclamations. The crucial point, however, is that all of us, whether we speak Greek or not, know what it sounded like when Odysseus, engaged in similar activities, called out the names of Penelope, Circe, Calypso, possibly Nausicaa, and (according to Kittler) the Sirens.

While trying to illustrate the basic operating principle of the Greek alphabet that "[e]ach simple sound is represented [. . .] by a single sign, and each sign always stands for the same sound," Ferdinand de Saussure, the eminent founder of modern linguistics, chose of all Greek words possible βάρβαρος (*bárbaros*) – an onomatopoetic word that imitates the incomprehensible noise emanating from the mouths of foreigners (see Saussure 1960: 39). Saussure is not known for his humor, but here he comes close to something resembling wit: the ingenuity of the Greek alphabet is exemplified by the discriminatory Greek term for those inferior souls that cannot speak (let alone write) Greek. The real hallmark of the Greek vowel alphabet is not that it allowed the Greeks to say clever things about themselves, but the fact that it allowed them to store barbarian babble as faithfully as it recorded their own elevated discourse. What sets the vowel alphabet apart, then, is the possibility of cross-cultural contact and appropriation rather than enhanced navel-gazing.

Just as Edison's phonograph records with equal impassivity Renfield's ramblings, Doctor Seward's analyses, and the rustling of oversized bats, and just as the computer indiscriminately processes noise and meaningful messages, the alphabet stores Plato as faithfully as the verbal hubbub of those whose writing systems cannot distinguish Plato from Pluto. This is the first hint at Kittler's grand historical arc that will link the Greek alphabet to the computer.

3. Of far greater consequence is the question of *why* the Greeks developed the vowel alphabet. Once again, the immediate answer is obvious: Phoenician is a Semitic, Greek an Indo-European language. Semitic languages are based on root consonants, which obviates the need for specific vowel signs, while Indo-European languages (and Greek in particular) make extensive use of vowels to indicate change of meaning. A sign system lacking vowels cannot adequately transcribe the latter. Κίρκη or Circe, the denouncer of the Sirens, can be rendered into Phoenician script, but not her island Aeaea.

But this explanation addresses constraint rather than cause; it helps explain why the Greeks were forced to develop a vowel alphabet, but it does not answer the question of why they developed such an alphabet in the first place. According to Kittler's grumpy assessment, there are "many lazy [*faule*] answers" (2006a: 110; note that German *faul* can also mean "rotten") which make reference to the mundane spheres of law, economy, and politics. By around 800 BCE the Greeks were venturing overseas, founding colonies, and involved in extensive trade with Eastern empires that were in possession of their own writing systems. So why not adapt a script and use it much like the trading partners were using theirs? The trouble is that "[u]nlike those of the Near East there is not a single archaic Greek inscription that deals with matters of trade, government or the law; they all emulate the

Odyssey by invoking wine, women and song" (Kittler 2006b: 55). Apart from a couple of proprietary inscriptions, short dedications and obscene graffiti, all the surviving fragments of early Greek writing are hexameters, some of them directly from the *Iliad* or the *Odyssey*. The classicist Barry Powell, who with regard to this particular issue is Kittler's principal authority, argues that the early alphabetic Greeks "act as if they know *only* how to write hexameters" (Powell 1991: 184). This comes as no surprise, for transcribing hexameters – and those of Homer in particular – was precisely what the new alphabet had been invented for in the first place.

> We cannot separate the invention of the alphabet from the recording of early hexametric poetry. We cannot separate the recording of early hexametric poetry from Homer. For extraordinary events we seek extraordinary causes. Homer sang his song and the adapter took him down. From this momentous event came classical Greek civilization and its achievements. But no achievement surpassed that of Homer and his scribe, who made Homer's song immortal. (Powell 1991: 237)

The notion that the Greek alphabet was fashioned in order to record hexametric verse had already peen proposed H. T. Wade-Gery in the late 1940s (Wade-Gery 1952: 11–14), though it remains a problematic hypothesis. As we shall see, in Kittler's case the controversy has less to do with whether or not this account is historically viable than with the underlying reasons why Kittler chose it.

4. But no matter how important the question of the origin of the Greek alphabet may be, the most pivotal issue is its subsequent refunctionalization. To be more precise: its unprecedented functional extension in the course of which signs representing phonetic elements also came to be used

as mathematical and as musical signs. Once again matters start out deceptively simply: "We exclusively call those scripts alphabets that, first, have a finite number of individual signs for all the sounds of a language, and, second, arrange these signs in a sequence" (Kittler 2006a: 105). Once this sequence is fixed it is easy to have a given element refer to its own numerical position in that sequence. Ordinal becomes cardinal: *Alpha* stands for the vowel *a*, but since it is firmly enshrined as the first letter in the mnemonic sequence *alpha-beta-gamma-delta* it can also stand for 1; in the same way β equals 2, γ equals 3, and so on. Two to three centuries after the introduction of the alphabet the numerical system appears to have been fully worked out. The first nine letters stood for 1 through 9, the second nine letters for the tens, and the third nine letters for the hundreds (since the Greek alphabet only had twenty-four letters three signs had to be added to arrive at the necessary twenty-seven numerals). Confusing letters and numerals was not a problem. "Whenever readers came across a sequence of letters which unlike all the others could not be translated into a sequence of sounds and thus into meaning or *logos*, it turned out to be a combination of hundreds, tens and ones, that is, a number" (Kittler 2006b: 56). Finally, "ever since Euripides the Greeks indicated [tones] with a letter from their alphabet rather than marking them, as we do, on staves" (Kittler 2006b: 56). One and the same sign system, then, was used for letters, numbers, and tones; and this came about because a sign system extended its function by using its own sequence. "Thus for the first time in the history of writing a set of signs was applied to itself; it was recoded" (Kittler 2006a: 208).

The latter is a crucially important point. Kittler is fascinated by the way in which the multi-functionality of the Greek alphabet arises from self-recursive operations. By exploiting its own properties one and the same sign system comes to indicate letters, numbers, and musical tones. To be sure, this is much more apparent (and systematic) in the case of sequenced letters turning into numbers, which is why Kittler is ultimately more interested in this refunctionalization of letters than in their (comparatively unsystematic) refunctionalization into tones. However, what is most intriguing to him is when numbers are used in a musical context. To be precise: when numbers are used to produce musical harmonies while playing a lyre. Referring to one of the key players in *Musik und Mathematik*, the Pythagorean philosopher Philolaus (approx. 470–385 BCE), Kittler explains that

> in order to teach singers and musicians by what stretch they had to shorten the string of their lyre in order to sound the fourth instead of the keynote, Philolaus simply put down δ καὶ γ: Strike the string at the point that marks the ratio four to three! (2006b: 56)

Kittler's argument is based on the premise that the lyre is *not* to be regarded as a simple musical tool or instrument. It is "a magical thing that connects mathematics to the domain of the senses" (2006b: 56), because it allows for the sensual (spoken words and songs) and the symbolic (a multi-functional, self-recursive sign system that provides exact instructions where to strike, how to sing, and what to recite) to be directly translated into each other. You do not perform a poem, song, or epic with the help of a lyre or a cithara in order to reveal its fundamental truths (let alone the fabled dialectic of enlightenment); it is through this performance that the audience may come to understand how signs and sense and their mutual interaction work. For Kittler, as we shall see in the concluding section, all the glory that was Greece resides *in the conscious performance of this alpha-numerical recursion* – a recursion that ties together signs,

senses, and sex in ways only certain Greeks were capable
of.

3. AND THE GODS MADE LOVE: PYTHAGOREAN GROUPIES

Have another look at the Sirens' greeting:

deur' ag' iôn, poluain' Oduseu, mega kudos Achaiôn

For Kittler, this is the most beautiful of the tens of thousands
of lines flowing from Homer's mouth. "Lovingly, all the
seven vowels and diphthongs known to the Greeks change in
the first verse, each time with only one mute sound in the syl-
lable. No verse was ever sung, no verse was ever repeated so
melodiously" (2006a: 51). Leaving aside the fact that Greek
has more diphthongs, the thrust of the argument is clear: this
is the most beautiful line because it is the most performative
– that is to say, the most evocative of the underlying rules
that govern both its production and transcription. Just as
"Brain Damage" foregrounds and thematizes the enraptur-
ing recording technology behind Pink Floyd's *Dark Side
of the Moon*, and just as Goethe's "Wanderer's Nightsong"
restages the hermeneutic *ur*-scene of Romantic poetry, this
line performs and highlights the constituent components
of the Greek language as well as that of its new recording
system. It is, as it were, a self-conscious celebration of the
Greek vowel alphabet at the time of its birth from the spirit
of hexametric poetry. But it is also as much a call to listen
(and leave the boat) as it is to love and learn.

First, the learning. The Sirens claim that they know "all
that comes to pass on the fertile earth." As Kittler points out
with palpable contempt (see 2006a: 55), Horkheimer and
Adorno based their reading of this passage on the influential

Homer translation by Johann Heinrich Voss (1751–1826), who rendered the last line as *alles, was irgend* geschah *auf der viel ernährenden Erde* – "all that *came* to pass on the fertile earth." The incorrect use of the past tense (which has been corrected in many subsequent editions), in combination with Horkheimer and Adorno's lack of familiarity with the Greek original, facilitated their philosophically embellished phantom sketch of the Sirens as beings exclusively associated with a primitive past and intent on subjecting Odysseus to irreversible regression (see Horkheimer and Adorno 1972: 33). Kittler, by contrast, agrees with Pucci's translation that the Sirens "know whatever happens" (2006a: 55; see also Pucci 1998: 1). Indeed, so full of knowledge are the Sirens that with the exception of omniscient Olympian deities such as Athene they are the only beings Odysseus encounters on his homeward journey who instantly recognize him. His wife Penelope and his servants do not, and neither do immortal beings like Circe and the Cyclops Polyphemus (and this despite the fact that both had been advised of his coming). By emphasizing their omniscience, Kittler is following a long-established tradition that identifies the Sirens with the Muses, the divine sources of knowledge and artistic inspiration. As Muses, the Sirens have a lot to offer, including such profound insight into "all that comes to pass on the fertile earth" that every visitor will leave their island a "wiser man."

What is intriguing from a media-historical point of view – especially a media history that tends to make of humans temporary junctures and inscription sites in the grand recursions of technological evolution – is the mythological association of the Muses with the introduction of writing. One version attributes the invention of the alphabet to the Phoenician immigrant Cadmus, founder of Thebes, who was given the hand of Aphrodite's daughter Harmonia in marriage and at whose wedding the Muses themselves, led by Apollo, provided the musical entertainment. In an alternate version the fashioning of the alphabet is the work of the Greek hero Palamedes, a man of such outstanding mental gifts that he even managed to outsmart the wily Odysseus (whereupon the latter had him framed as a traitor to the Greek cause and put to death). In an intriguing paean, the Greek writer Philostratus hailed Palamedes as the "author of the Muses" (Philostratus 2005: 373), which leaves open whether Palamedes was inspired by the Muses or whether he, by virtue of his invention of the alphabet, had a hand in creating them. The ritual invocation of the Muses takes on a special note when it is linked to the introduction of memorization techniques whose storage capabilities outstrip those of the individual bard – as expressed by Homer at the outset of the famous Catalogue of Ships passage in the second book of the *Iliad*:

> Sing to me now, you Muses, who hold the halls of
>   Olympus!
> You are goddesses, you are everywhere. You know all
>   things –
> all we hear is the distant ring of glory, we know
>   nothing –
> who were the captains of Achaea? Who were the
>   kings?
> The mass of troops I cold never tally, never name,
> not even if I had ten tongues and ten mouths,
> a tireless voice and the heart inside me bronze,
> never unless you Muses of Olympus, daughters of
>   Zeus,
> whose shield is rolling thunder, sing, sing in memory
> all who gathered under Troy. (Homer 1996: 115)

Together with many other similar invocations this passage – which according to Kittler is later bowdlerized into

Christian fantasy in St Paul's I Corinthians 13 ("Though I speak with the tongues of men and of angels") – celebrates the close association of storage and inspiration. It is nothing less than a Homeric discourse on discourse channel conditions. By inviting and willingly submitting to a force of song and memory superior to his own, the bard is welcoming that take-over of tongue and mind described in Pink Floyd's "Brain Damage": *There's someone in my head but it's not me.*

Second, the love. *Deur' ag' iôn*, the Sirens sing – come here. Before and beyond all learned exegesis, it is an invitation to have sex. On this fairly accessible level of analysis the Sirens are nymphs (or, to quote Vladimir Nabokov's *Lolita*, nymphets) rather than Muses, and the passage devoted to them appears to be the straightforward tale of a couple of girls hanging out on the beach waiting for a sailor willing to have a good time. He arrives, disembarks, they make love, he replenishes his water supplies, and sails on, though in order to ensure that what happens on Li Galli stays on Li Galli he later concocts tall tales of danger and self-negation that for millennia will fool his audiences, up to and including the gullible hobby philosophers of the Frankfurt School. In a next step, this reading is granted an etymological halo. Proving once again that he is willing to rush in where experts fear to tread, Kittler rejects all alternate explanations of the origin of *siren* (for instance, that it derives from *seira*, the Greek word for rope, or from the star Sirius) and opts for a Thracian origin, according to which *zeirênê* refers to Aphrodite, who is of course the goddess of the love that the sirens are offering to Odysseus.

Not coincidentally, the first book of the first volume of *Musik und Mathematik* is named *Aphrodite*. As an object of investigation and a subject of inspiration, she appears to be very much on Kittler's mind. Cutting a swathe through

the Classics of Greek literature, he scours text after text in
search of similar invocations of, or invitations to and by,
this particular goddess. Homer had provided a couple of
Olympian *ur*-scenes: "Quick, my darling, come, let's go to
bed / And lose ourselves in love!" (Homer 1996: 200) are
the words used by Ares to seduce his half-sister Aphrodite
while her husband Hephaistos is off on business. They are
repeated almost verbatim by the duped and lust-filled Zeus –
"Come, let's go to bed, let's lose ourselves in love!" (Homer
1991: 380) – when catching sight of his wife and sister Hera
wearing Aphrodite's irresistible girdle. "Come hither, if ever
before thou didst hear my voice afar," Sappho sings in her
beautiful Hymn to Aphrodite, and even in the tragic depths
of Sophocles' *Oedipus at Colonus* the chorus invokes the
"Goddess Aphrodite, the charioteer with the golden reins of
love" (Sophocles 1984: 326).

What is at stake here is nothing less than the attempt to
recoup what Kittler considers the original Greek meaning
of *mimesis* – an endeavor that takes on almost anthropologi-
cal proportions. The basic idea seems to be that whenever
Greeks made love with reference to their gods – for instance,
when during some festival the country lads and lasses dressed
up as Dionysos and Aphrodite and frolicked on the pastures
(which is how, according to Aristotle, Homer was conceived)
– they were mimicking the preferred behavior of their gods
and thus re-creating their own origin. At rock bottom, Greek
song and poetry, before it descended into the realms of mere
literature, celebrated the joyful acts of unencumbered love
and their constant reiterations:

> The chain of these repetitions [. . .] transforms love into
> song. And for a good reason, indeed for the best in the
> world: Without gods making love there would be no mor-
> tals, without parents making love there would be none of

us children. Thus only gratitude and repetition remain. As long as the Greeks were singing rather than perpetrating speeches or literature, this was the meaning of μίμησις, dance as an imitation of the gods. And the gods made love. (Kittler 2006a: 128).

Or, with telegraphic economy: "Gods lead the way making love, we mortals follow. And that is mimesis, nothing else" (2006a: 127). The opening line of the Siren song, then, not only consciously repeats and performs the techniques and sign systems on which it passed, it also, and equally consciously, repeats the invitation to perform the acts of love that are then praised (frequently in order to incite further repetitions) in countless songs and epics.

Here, a certain ontological whiff enters Kittler's deliberations, in the guise of the Pythagorean teachings of Philolaus and others. Just as living beings are made, very literally, by a coupling of male and female, the world arises from odd and even. Ratios that (re)produce the harmony of sound are numerical relationships making love: "Listen to the voice of bright muses. Think the world (with or without Philolaus) as simple as it is: made of women and men" (2006a: 171). Sirens and lyres sing *of* love (and frequently lead to love-making) and they *are* love, for generating signs, sounds, and children all arise from the recursive operation of basic constituent elements that belong to two separate groups: even numbers, consonants, and men on the one side and odd numbers, vowels, and women on the other. It just takes one party – for instance, Odysseus' groupies on Li Gallo – to call out *deur' ag' iôn*.

For those who object to the word *groupie*: have another look at the longer quote above. The final sentence "and the Gods made love" appears in English in Kittler's German text. It is a quote – one of many quotes that reveal Kittler's desire to enrich his particular construction of ancient Greece with countercultural aspirations from the 1960s. "And the Gods made love" is the title of the psychedelic lead-off track on Jimi Hendrix' legendary 1968 album *Electric Ladyland*. Kittler, an avid Hendrix fan, is playing with several Hendrix myths. Some claim that "electric ladies" are groupies (which makes sense given that *Electric Ladyland* was dedicated to them), while others insist that Hendrix was referring to guitars. The superimposition of guitars and groupies indicates the way sex and music – the exploration of love and harmonies – merged in Kittler's Greece, as they probably also did for Jimi.

4. GREEK-GERMAN AFFAIRS

Whether or not there really was a Homer, whether or not the vowel alphabet was indeed designed to transcribe his epics, whether or not the *Iliad* and the *Odyssey* really are each divided into twenty-four books because the Greek alphabet has twenty-four letters (see Kittler 2006a: 120), whether or not Kittler's treatment of Philolaus and others is based on selective and dubious readings of a few surviving fragments – all this and much more will have to be addressed by experts. (So far, their feedback has not been very encouraging.) Amateurs should stick to what they do best: replace informed discussions of technical and historical details with generalizations that dwell on trends and motives. In this spirit we may ask: what kind of a Greece does Kittler envision, and why?

1. Kittler's Greece is a very *isolated* affair. Many experts, including Walter Burkert, one of Kittler's principal sources, emphasize the "cultural continuum" that in the days of Homer extended "over the entire Mediterranean" (Burkert 1992: 128), but Kittler turns Greece into a culturally

self-enclosed region whose emergence required little inter-
cultural exchange. Burkert asserts that the "Greek miracle"
is not merely the result of a "unique talent" but also "owes
its existence to the simple phenomenon that the Greeks are
the most easterly of Westerners" (Burkert 1992: 129); Kittler
draws a clear line between (European) Greeks on the one
hand and (Asian) Persians, Semites, or Egyptians on the
other. Not to mention his disdain for their inferior Western
neighbors who, in one of his latest mantras, are routinely
dismissed as *die dummen Römer* – the silly Romans.

2. Kittler's Greece is a very *cultural* affair. To claim that
the invention of the vowel alphabet arose from the desire to
transcribe Homer's epics, rather than from any need to take
stock of governmental or economic activities, serves to re-
inscribe the traditional image of ancient Greece as first and
foremost a cultural entity. After all (so the venerable story
goes) antiquity never knew a state or a politically or economically united entity called Greece; rather, there was at
best a highly divisive patchwork of city-states and kingdoms,
of democracies, aristocracies, and tyrannies, that appeared to
share a common language and culture. By combining Greek
isolation and the primacy of culture "Kittler *de facto* estab-
lishes a realm of cultural purity" (Breger 2006: 125). No
need, therefore, to consider inferior neighbors or the messy
netherworld of trade and politics.

3. Kittler's Greece is a very *German* affair. The media-
historical resonance – that is, the idea that the digitally
enhanced re-appearance of a multi-functional sign system
facilitates a greater understanding of the original Greek
alphanumeric achievement – is a technologically informed
variation of a peculiar notion that occasionally haunts certain
sections of classical studies: namely, that there are times, countries, and regions that share a deeper spiritual connection with
ancient Greece and are therefore more privy to the secrets of

antiquity. Germans who spend a lot of time exploring ancient Greece appear to be especially prone to this perception of cultural affinity. The most prominent protagonist was, no doubt, Heidegger, who could on occasion wax mysteriously about the deep ties between language and thought that characterize both Greek and German. This focus on linguistic affinity grew out of a perceived historical similarity, for until 1871 Germany was, as it were, a colder and woodier Greece north of the Alps. Just like Greece, Germany was for a very long time a frequently highly divisive patchwork of city-states, petty duchies, and kingdoms that shared a common language and that subsequently came to see itself in the first instance as a cultural rather than a political or economic entity. (And just like Greece its fate was often linked to intrusions from empires located to the East and West.) This primacy of cultural production is at the heart of the so-called "Tyranny of Greece over Germany" (Butler 1935), and its most conspicuous linguistic residue is the distinctly German compound noun *Kulturnation* ("culture-nation").

There is a form of narcissism at work here. Once German writers and philosophers praise Greece *and* establish the alleged linguistic, cultural, or spiritual affinity, all that is praiseworthy about the Greeks also applies to the Germans. Talking about Greece was a way Germans could practice self-idealization without talking about themselves:

> [I]dealization is by no means the expression of astonishment, of reverence, of surprise and of adoration of the Other, but the transference of the ideal German image most of these authors (even if not all) entertained about themselves to the ancient Greeks. By inscribing their identity on the body of the Greeks, German writers and philosophers constructed their own ideal types and, like Narcissus, fell in love with themselves in the garment of Greeks. (Heller 2008: 55)

In her incisive critique of Kittler's "philhellenic fantasies," Claudia Breger argues that he "returns to concepts and fantasies articulated in the 19th- and early 20th-century phil-hellenic thinking, but [. . .] these moves are driven by late 20th-century feedback" (Breger 2006: 114). That is to say, Kittler does not simply rehash philhellenic notions that were grounded in the German self-affirmations of the nineteenth century or in the cultural unrest of the Weimar Republic; his notion of Greek cultural purity clearly builds on these tradi-tions and then uses them as part of a projection screen for the renegotiation of German national identity in the post-unification age. To emphasize that Greece is neither Eastern (Asian) nor Western (Roman) but its own master, is to tackle in antique disguise the vexing problem (which was also much on the mind of Heidegger) as to what degree Germany is able, maybe even destined, to find a third way that avoids the capitalist (American), communist (Russian), or – to update the equation – radical Islamic aberrations. As Kittler claimed in a recent interview, as an extension of *Discourse Networks* his Greek project aims to "provide Europe – also in the interest of Europe – with a viable foundation of thought and to return to the Greeks. After all, do we want to end up in the New Testament, the Old Testament, or the Koran? For heaven's sake: No!" (Kittler and Weinberger 2009: 93). All this involves an irritating terminological superimposition: it is at times difficult to avoid the suspicion that – probably in order to avoid suspect chauvinism – Kittler sometimes uses "Europe" when he means "Germany." No doubt Kittler's Greece is not only a retrojected Germany but also a stand-in for a (culturally superior) Europe sandwiched between (cul-turally inferior) neighboring empires

4. Regardless of his reverential treatment of Sappho, Kittler's idealized early Greece is a very *heteronormative* affair. But somehow it did not last; a pristine aphroditic world of

letters, lyres, and theo-mimetic lovemaking was afflicted by
a reduction of elementary heterosexual vigor. Increasingly,
Greeks make words rather than love; and Kittler appears to
lament this flagging of priapic juices. In this particular context, Breger has zeroed in on a revealing difference between
Kittler and Foucault as regards their readings of Plato's
Symposium. For Kittler, the refusal of Socrates to sleep with
Alcibiades signals a decline in which mere speech comes
to replace *Rausch* or intoxication (see Kittler and Vismann
2001: 86), whereas for Foucault precisely the opposite was
the case: "Within his system of cultural codes, Socrates' sov-
ereign ability to renounce what he *does* desire is the basis
for his masculinity" (Breger 2006: 123). This practice of
self-negation for the purpose of building up inner reserves
(which was also central to the reading of the *Odyssey* proposed
by Horkheimer and Adorno) is linked to a reorientation
toward homosexual relationships in what Kittler calls "the
age of classical pederasty" (Kittler and Vismann 2001: 80).
Breger pinpoints this association as particularly problematic
in Kittler's narrative, for it appears to reiterate "stereotypical connotations of male homosexuality with emasculation"
(Breger 2006: 123). Those who can, do; those who no longer
want to do what they can, teach. Once again, the shadow of
Nietzsche looms large: Socrates, the first philosopher, is also
the first decadent.

5. Kittler's Greece is a rather *non-poststructuralist* affair.
The departure from Foucault in sexual matters is yet another
instance of Kittler's increasing distance from the Parisian
master thinkers he is invariably associated with. While
Kittler would never dream of bestowing upon Foucault the
choice epithets he reserves for Horkheimer and Adorno, it
is difficult to avoid the conclusion that his Greek work is as
incompatible with Foucault's *History of Sexuality* as it is with
the *Dialectic of Enlightenment.* Breger is right to surmise that

Foucault must be spinning in his grave apropos of the way Kittler practically inverts Foucault's analysis of the Greek complicity of sexuality and subjectivity (see Breger 2006: 120). Lacan, the great guest in Freiburg, doesn't fare any better. Kittler's emphasis on fullness, plenitude, and performative presence in his idealized Greece is very much at odds with Lacan's insistence on lack and deferral. As Breger points out, this puts Kittler closer to his arch-enemies in Frankfurt than to his masters in Paris:

> [Kittler's] romantic fantasy of a divine fullness unmarked by differences resonates with the programmatically anti-repressive developments of psychoanalysis generally associated with the student movement of 1968 and left-wing politics in its wake. Kittlers' thinking thus joins forces with some of his favorite opponents in German academia, including Herbert Marcuse, who re-centered Heidegger's ontology of ecstasy around the sexual theme omitted by the master himself. (Breger 2006: 122–3).

These Greek departures from Foucault and Lacan are part of an epic occidental overview that defies some of the most basic tenets of so-called poststructuralism. To use the most glaring example, as already mentioned, Kittler alludes to a certain similarity between the Greek alphanumerical system and the computer. Both are based on recursively operating sign systems that can process linguistic, visual, and acoustic data. Of course, Kittler is not so naive as to propose that the lyre is a universal machine, or that Philolaus is Alan Turing in a toga, but he clearly insinuates a cyclical or spiraling structure in as far as the digital code echoes the multi-functional Greek alphabet on a higher level. "In the Greek alphabet our senses were present – and thanks to Turing they are so *once again*" (2006b: 59; emphasis added). Or, even more clearly: "The alphabet of the Greeks fuses image, writing and number for a long time [. . .] Only we, who after so much going astray have landed in Turing's wondrous galaxy, where scripts, images and tones consist of 0 and 1, only we are able to grasp what that means" (2006a: 207). The crux of the matter is that *media-historical resonance has a profound cognitive impact*. We are able to grasp what happened in Greece because "for the second time in history, a universal medium of binary numbers is able to encode, to transmit and to store whatever will happen, from writing or counting to imaging or sounding" (Kittler 2009: 24). Because of the return of self-recursive multi-functionality under digital conditions we are in a privileged position to understand the culture of ancient Greece better than preceding generations, and maybe even better than the Greeks themselves did.

What we have here is another manifestation of a pan-occidental Hegelian chronicle that defies the orthodox distrust of grand narratives promulgated by poststructuralists. Foucauldian ruptures yield to Hegelian vistas; fractured voices give way to elementary fullness; plenitude replaces lack; constant deferral is sidelined by the possibility of a new beginning. Yet, despite all this, Kittler is stuck with the poststructuralist label. In a recent essay on Pynchon's *Gravity's Rainbow* Kittler ridiculed the arbitrary use of the term "postmodern," whose main function appears to be to allow scholars to avoid dealing with the (weapons-)technological aspects of the novel "in the face of which the traditional tools of our Humanities fail miserably" (Kittler 2003b: 123). Doesn't the same apply to "poststructuralism"? Maybe the term is not quite as threadbare, but in the face of Kittler's Greek excursions the onus is on those who still affix the label to explain what they mean by it.

7. Ultimately Kittler's Greece is a very *media-theoretical* affair. Any student of media theory knows that media shifts

and the habituation to new media technologies inevitably give rise to new understanding of media history. No doubt digital technologies will reshape our view of Homer, which was already fundamentally changed by the introduction of analog storage devices. The formulation of the so-called Oral Formulaic Hypothesis proposed by Milman Parry and Albert Lord, according to which Homer's style is characterized by the extensive use of epithetic formulas and fixed expressions, is directly linked to the introduction of phonography, that is, to the new possibilities of recording and transcribing Homer's modern European counterparts, the bards of Serbia and Croatia. "'Primary orality;' and 'oral history' came into existence only after the end of the writing monopoly, as the technological shadow of the apparatuses that document them" (Kittler 1999: 7). Media theory and communication studies have their own changing media-technological a priori.

But our understanding of past media achievements is as much affected by present media performances as it is by associated projections. Given the unrivaled status of ancient Greece as a cultural reference point where – in the words of a famous British Graecophile – "grew the arts of war and peace," it comes as no surprise that we not only grant it a paradigmatic status in the realms of politics, philosophy, and the art of fighting in a phalanx, but also view it as a model of communicative dynamics. The latter is most clearly on display in the work of Innis. While Kittler's early, musico-mathematical Greece is a projection of (counter) cultural agendas that are directed against the academic and political mainstream, Innis's idealization of ancient Athenian Greece as a place which achieved a balance between time- and space-based media is a projection arising from fears over a forgetfulness of time and tradition in a world buried under an onslaught of (electric and electronic) space-biased communication technologies. And, just as Kittler's Greece stands for a Germany or Europe able to disentangle itself from the encroaching tentacles of neighboring empires, Innis's Greece is what Canada could or should be in the face of American hegemony. Both Kittler's and Innis's Greece are large-scale survival scenarios: Kittler's Greece can be a model for how Europe can teach the world something by exhibiting what it learned about itself; Innis's Greece is a model of how "Canada was to play Athens to the Rome of the United States" (Kroker 1984: 117). All (Western) countries, it appears, are Greek, but some are a bit more Greek than others.

5. GREEK STAKES: THE MEANING OF BEING

All this comes with one important caveat: Kittler's Greece is a highly selective, internally *divided* affair. His Greece is not that of coffee-table books, documentaries, and world literature reading courses; it is not the Greece of Pericles or Plato, the Parthenon or the *polis*. In a word, Kittler's Greece (unlike that of Innis and most other Graecophiles) *is not Athens*. In ways that, once again, have their roots in an intellectual tradition that reaches as far back as the German Romantics and that pass through Nietzsche and Heidegger (who could almost be listed as co-authors of *Musik und Mathematik*), the differentiation between Greece and its inferior neighbors is re-entered *within* Greece. Kittler's idealized Greece is that of Homer and Hesiod, Sappho and Sophocles (as opposed to the misogynist Euripides, whom Kittler thrashes with the abandon he normally reserves for members of the Frankfurt School). We are dealing with another episode in the love affair between Germany and the Presocratics, that is, with a peculiar predilection exhibited by a number of German philosophers for early Greek singers and thinkers, most of whom did not reside in Athens and/or lived prior to the crucial divide that – to use Heidegger's biased binary – replaced thought and poetry (*Denken und Dichten*) with mere philosophy and literature (for a detailed study, see Bambach 2005). Kittler's special twist is to add Pythagoreans like Philolaus to the equation, whom Heidegger did not fully appreciate, but the basic diagnosis remains the same: something happened around the fourth century BCE in Greece – something went wrong; a promising beginning was aborted, and it is vital that we understand and reconnect with those pristine days.

From Kittler's point of view, this crucial divide occurred when the conscious, celebratory, and media-based performance of the interaction between signs and senses was replaced by an ontological stew that, more or less oblivious of its technological conditions, proceeded to analyze the world according to "form and matter, meaning and non-meaning, spirit and body and all the other absurdities that have been around since 330 B.C.E." (Kittler 2006b: 55). Instead of celebration, conscious re-enactment, and intransitivity, we find philosophically embellished denigration, forgetfulness, and hermeneutics. The celebration of elementary matters such as song, speech, and numbers (not to mention food and water) turns into their denigration as they are now used in purely instrumental fashion to refer to philosophical or scientific truths. Existence as a conscious re-enactment of divine acts that brought us into being yields to a forgetfulness of that which is, at best, unconsciously repeated. Finally, the recursivity of medial performances – lovingly singing and speaking about the ways we sing, speak, and love – gives way to the subordination of medium to message. To put it bluntly, Kittler's idealized Greece appears to have been one big discourse on discourse channel conditions. All of the early Greek bards and mathematicians are singing "Brain

Damage," as it were, though in a decidedly Heideggerian vein:

> The meaning of being is that there is being. Whoever hopes for more is deluded. Homer sung it for us. His legends were written down from the very beginning. That separates Being [*Sein*], as it once arose in the dawn of Greece, from all the scraps of prose the many other, equally old legends of Troy and Thebes turned into (sometimes not until one millennium later).
>
> The singer sings; enchanted, we listen. The singer sings that his hero, too, enchants all his listeners when he sings. One, male or female, wrote along with the singer. And that was it. (2006a: 121)

From Being to scraps of prose; from the enchantment of the rose-colored dawn of Greece to the grey of the never-ending labor of misguided interpretation – we are dealing with the story of an epochal rupture in the Heideggerian history of being (*Seinsgeschichte*) that served to enthrone millennia of hermeneutic aberration. A story like this is in need of heroes (Kittler is inclined to nominate Homer, the Pythagoreans, Heidegger, and himself), but more importantly it needs the right villain. Kittler has a worthy candidate in mind: Aristotle.

Aristotle's teacher Plato – another suspect Athenian involved in the destruction of Nietzsche's, Heidegger's, and Kittler's Presocratic, non-Athenian Greece – had already initiated the divide between matter and mathematics by eschewing the strong Pythagorean complicity of numbers and being in favor of his more abstract notion of ideas. As Eric Havelock emphasized, the latter reveals the profound impact of increased alphabetization on the discursive practices of classical Athens. The stability, retrievability, and communicability facilitated by phonetic transcription were transferred from concrete word to abstract thing. Ideas are a glorified abstraction of writing practices; only when writing is part of social reality can there be an ideal, higher, realm of enduring truths, a realm more real than the reality it both denies and depends on. In a Kittlerian vein, Alfred North Whitehead's famous claim that European philosophical tradition "consists of a series of *footnotes* to Plato" (1978: 39; emphasis added) must be read literally rather than metaphorically. With Plato, philosophy comes into being as writing; any subsequent contribution – be it for or against Plato – cannot be anything but a further instance of writing.

All this boils down to one basic fact: philosophy – as opposed to what Heidegger called *Denken* (thinking) – is based on the suppression of the very medium that gave rise to it. If the latter is acknowledged at all, this is only in metaphorical fashion, as in the famous passage on writing in Plato's *Phaedrus*. As Kittler argues in his essay "Towards an Ontology of Media," the inability of philosophy to

> conceive of media as media [. . .] begins with Aristotle: first, because his ontology deals only with things, their matter and form, but not with relations between things in time and space. [. . .] Second, because the Greeks did not distinguish between articulated speech elements and articulated alphabetic letters, the very concept of writing as philosophy's own (technical) medium is missing from Aristotle onwards. (2009: 23–4).

The Greek alphabet was a bit too efficient; it was so good it became true. The ease with which letters came to serve speech made it easy to forget the former over the latter. Ignoring the highly effective, and therefore almost invisible medium he relied on, Aristotle's metaphysics came to center on the distinction between *eidos* and *hule*, form and matter, an unequal binary that presupposes a form of presence or immediacy that categorically denies the spatial deferrals involved in mediating the object under investigation. The irony, however, is that for all his marginalization of mediality Aristotle was among the first to conceive of media, though he did so exclusively in the context of human sensory perception. Prior to Aristotle, Kittler argues, the Greek atomists had maintained that, in order to see something small, images or *eidola* detach themselves from a given object and travel through a vacuum until they meet our eyes. Not so, Aristotle opined; between us and the objects there is air and inside our eyes there is water, both of which have to be traversed. Hence water and air imply a "between," that is, a medium:

> In other words, he [Aristotle] is the fist to turn a common Greek preposition – *metaxú*, between – into a philosophical noun or concept: *tò metaxú*, the medium. "In the middle" of absence and presence, farness and nearness, being and soul, there exists no nothing anymore, but a media relation. (Kittler 2009: 26)

It's not quite that simple. For one, the translation or identification of *tò metaxú* with Latin *medium* first occurs in Thomas of Aquinas' rather liberal Latin rendition (*De Anima*) of Aristotle's *Peri Psyches*, and whether it is due to Aquinas' shaky command of Greek or the impact of his own preconceived notions, what he calls *medium* is not identical with Aristotle's "between." Furthermore, a closer reading of *Peri Psyches* reveals that *tò metaxú* is not so much an original contribution by Aristotle as his paraphrase of the teachings of Democritus. *Tò metaxú* is not only that which is between object and eye; it is also that between the texts of Democritus and Aristotle (Hagen 2008: 23).

But the basic narrative remains unaffected by this. Aristotle emerges as a checkered villain of Shakespearian dimensions, who with an extraordinary mixture of blindness and insight brought about an epochal cover-up but who nonetheless also provided the key notions that would serve to uncover the suppressed. Philosophy in the classical sense of the word, and a media theory that is worth its name, are incompatible since the emergence of the former rested on the suppression of the latter. The recuperation of mediality proper, then, depends on overcoming metaphysical suppression, which, however, provides the entry point to its own supersession. That pivotal moment, Kittler continues, occurred – or began to occur – with Heidegger's de(con)struction of occidental metaphysics.

Kittler, then, clearly views his alphanumerical mega-project as a continuation of Heidegger's *Seinsgeschichte* or history of being, though in a technologically and mathematically more informed way. Like Heidegger, he goes back to the aborted beginnings of European thinking, but unlike Heidegger he reserves a special place for the practical performance of numbers facilitated by the recursions of the alphanumerical vowel alphabet, as is on display in Philolaus's lyre instruction δ και γ:

This instruction differs from the ontology of Aristotle in two elementary ways: First, it is without a doubt true; and second, it can effortlessly be proven. Whoever has ears to hear can simply follow Philolaus and discover that a lyre is not only a musical instrumental such as exists in any culture, but also a magical thing that connects mathematics to the domain of the senses; it is, to use Hans-Jörg Rheinberger's neologism, an "epistemic thing." Such manifestness appears to be the only meaning of meaning, that is, the only meaning that *logos* can take on under computerized condition. After all, Philolaus and his followers, the "so-called Pythagoreans" [. . .] literally referred to the 4:3 ratio of the fourth, the 3:2 ratio of the fifth, and 2:1 ratio of the octave as *logoi*. (Kittler 2006b: 56)

Logos is neither mere word nor grand abstract concept, but a harmony that enchants and that can be numerically analyzed. This allows us to cut to the core implications of Kittler's Greek venture:

1. Already in 1995 Kittler conceded that he "merely transferred Heidegger's concept of technology to media" (Kittler and Banz 1996: 21); and in a recent interview he offered the most economic summary of his work to date by labeling it "an up-to-date *Seinsgeschichte*, so to speak" (Kittler and Weinberger 2009: 102). This informed subservience to Heidegger now reappears as Kittler joins Heidegger in pronouncing the death of the latter's own discipline and the birth of something that both preceded and is poised to succeed it. The return to *a thinking in and of mediality* that was silenced by ontology spells the end of philosophy. If fundamental distinctions that are indispensable for the operations of philosophy such as the one between *physis* and *logos* break down because, as Heidegger was shocked to realize, the latter can now be performed by and inside machines, philosophy has come to an end:

> Insofar as Aristotelian logic is no professor's task anymore, but implemented in digital computers, philosophy as such has come to its historical end; at the same time, however, the dawn or task of thinking has barely begun. Heidegger asks us in simple words to rethink for the first time the media history of Europe as such, and this at the very moment when European thought disappears by its global expansion. The recursion should start with the earliest

Greek thinker-poets, pass to Aristotle's fatal distinction between physics and logic, and lead to our latest logical and arithmetical machinery. (Kittler 2009: 29)

The stakes are spelled out in the beginning of *Musik und Mathematik*: "Either a new beginning will succeed or that of Greece was in vain" (2006a: 12). To fail at the "new task of thinking" is tantamount to betraying Greece.

2. Provided that it ever had a beginning, so-called poststructuralism also comes to an end. It is no longer necessary to avoid Heidegger or to approach him in a roundabout way via Derrida, Lacan, or Foucault. If the older Heidegger had already come close to realizing the impact of digital technology that the younger Kittler was about to explore in greater detail, then there is little space left between them. But that was precisely the space in which "French theory" had acted as a bridge connecting Heidegger to those thinkers like Kittler who fully realized the conditions and implications of Heidegger's thought. It is not that Kittler abandons Lacan and Foucault; they merely vanish much like receding hills disappear into the (Black Forest) mountain range behind them. This is particularly obvious in the case of Foucault. On the one hand, Foucauldian discourse analysis, with its focus on ensembles of utterances that are not explored with a view to their meaning, but always against the sum total of what could have been said in a given episteme, points toward Shannon's information theory which states the information resides in the ratio between what is said and what could have been said. On the other hand, the Foucauldian history of ruptures is, to Kittler, ultimately nothing but a long footnote to Heidegger's equally rupture-prone *Seinsgeschichte* or history of being. In short, the poststructuralist intermediaries are absorbed by what came before and after them. Freiburg – the city of Heidegger and Kittler – can now indulge in

a conversation with itself; it no longer requires a Parisian detour.

3. Leaving aside all the philological, philosophical, media-theoretical, and musico-historical issues that require more detailed analysis, it is obvious that Kittler's Greece is a multifaceted projection. As Claudia Breger has analyzed, some are related to long-standing German philhellenic fantasies; others to countercultural aspirations of 1968. The latter, no doubt, come with a certain entertainment value. In an extensive review of *Musik und Mathematik* Larson Powell chastised Kittler's style as "Heidegger for hippies" (Powell 2008: 95); this is also an apt summary of the content: Kittler's Greece is made up of Heidegger *and* the hippies. But his Greece is also a projection screen for something else: himself. His Greece is an idealized self-portrait of Peloponnesian proportions. Under their serene Mediterranean sky these Greeks are doing what he sees himself doing. Listening to Homer, Sappho, or the Sirens, they are enraptured, intoxicated, spellbound; taking lyre and wax tablet in hand, they work out how those enchantments came about and how they can be repeated. Kittler, in turn, reads Hegel and Foucault, Homer and Pynchon; he listens to Wagner and Ligeti, Jimi Hendrix and Pink Floyd, and is enraptured; then he proceeds to locate the discursive rules – in time, the appropriate term will be algorithms – that programmed texts and intoxications, and he will build the machines and write the codes that give rise to the enchantment. This is probably the most fundamental feature of Kittler's work, the constant transition *between rapture and rule analysis.* And just like the happy Greeks in the days before the philosopher spoilsports came along and extricated message and meaning from media and performance, Kittler refuses to succumb to hermeneutic temptations, just as he later refuses to betray the hardware for something delusional conjured up by the software. After being over-

whelmed by "Brain Damage" and comparable events, it becomes imperative to study how the song inflicts its title on listeners by building machines that disclose the rules of such an infection:

> In the case of my generation, whose ears were full of Hendrix crashes and Pink Floyd and who were overwhelmed and completely awed, I tried to move back from these blissful shocks in such a way as at least to be able to build technical apparatuses according to plan that were themselves capable of performing these feats. That, after all, is the only way one can deal with art. (Kittler and Maresch 1994: 107)

5

CONTROVERSIAL ACHIEVEMENTS

1. "MEDIA DETERMINE OUR SITUATION"

Kittler is controversial. That, probably, is the only uncontroversial thing that can be said about him. To exacerbate matters, it is difficult to distinguish between genuine and gratuitous controversies. Some debates, including those focusing on Kittler's blunders and questionable assumptions, are no doubt necessary, but others are not, particularly those that use Kittler as a convenient stand-in for larger debates surrounding poststructuralism, anti-humanism, or technodeterminism. In addition, there is a sizeable group of superfluous controversies that focus with great gusto and indignation on provocative asides and one-liners that Kittler never meant seriously (though critics rightly object to the fact that he launched them in the first place). Any final assessment of Kittler, therefore, must contain a review of controversial points.

To begin with, there is the inevitable charge of technodeterminism, an accusation that frequently contains a whiff of moral indignation. To label someone a technodeterminist is a bit like saying that he enjoys strangling cute puppies: the depraved wickedness of the action renders further discussion unnecessary. There is no shortage of critics – many of whom appear to lack either the talent or the time to specify what exactly they mean by technodeterminism – who are not interested in pursuing the matter any further; they just want to make the label stick and move on.

To be sure, the accusation is anything but unfounded. Blanket statements like "[m]edia determine our situation" (Kittler 1999: xxxix) deserve equally apodictic rejoinders. Problems, however, arise once you take a closer look at some of Kittler's historical analyses. The switch from the Discourse Network 1800 to the Discourse Network 1900, no doubt, is said to be caused by a media shift. With the arrival of new technological means of processing data, the whole cultural superstructure is overturned. But what about the preceding shift from the so-called Scholar's Republic (which is Kittler's version of the "classical" episteme depicted in Foucault's *Order of Things*) to the Discourse Network 1800? There was no corresponding media rupture in the second half of the eighteenth century. The discursive, educational, and governmental practices changed, but the data-processing technologies remained the same. Kittler is saying what he does not like to say: the codes and protocols that make people speak and write in new ways originated primarily in the social rather than the technological realm.

Media-theoretical introductions and handbooks love to pair up Kittler with that other famed technodeterminist, Marshall McLuhan. There are obvious parallels and influences. Both were scholars of literature who, dissatisfied with their discipline, came to engage the structures and effects of changing media technologies; and in both cases it was precisely their philological background that enabled their impact on media studies. In terms of methodology and material, *Gramophone, Film, Typewriter* and *Optical Media* owe far more to *Understanding Media* than the occasional (and occasionally ridiculing) references to McLuhan indicate. Not to mention the similarity of tone; as John Peters remarks, Kittler is closer to "McLuhan's flamboyant vaticism than to Innis's cranky accumulation of detail" (2010: 6). To this day, Kittler still likes to quote McLuhan, but it is obvious that he thinks of him as someone who identified the right problems but kept coming up with the wrong explanations. Unlike McLuhan, Kittler does not feel the need to squeeze all of media through the bottleneck of the human sensory apparatus, which, as James Carey pointed out decades ago, "is a very weak foundation to support such a vast superstructure" (Carey 1969: 294). McLuhan's focus on human perceptions is tied to the fundamental difference between him and Kittler. In the latter's words, McLuhan "understood more about perception than electronics, and therefore he attempted to think about technology in terms of bodies instead of the other way round" (2010: 29). In short, McLuhan was and remains an anthropocentric thinker who conceptualizes media as extensions of the human body; to rid himself of this fallacy he should either have studied more electronics or read more Heidegger. Besides, McLuhan was an enthusiastic Catholic, and for the Protestant Kittler McLuhan's exuberant notion that the computer will usher in "a Pentecostal condition of universal understanding and unity" (McLuhan 1964: 83) is nothing but an "arch-catholic media cult, which simply confuses the Holy Spirit and Turing's machine" (Kittler 2010: 30).

But there is a more subtle difference that cuts to the core of the technodeterminist issue. According to McLuhan, the technological qualities of a given medium affect in predictable manner the sense ratio and hence alter the individual as well as perception. The sequential linearity of typography, for instance, already entails the detached, eye-centered, objective world of the Gutenberg galaxy. This facet of technodeterminism is absent from Kittler's more subtle account. As the non-technological shift from the Scholar's Republic to the Discourse Network 1800 indicates, Kittler instead posits a far more contingent relationship between technology and mindset. It is more revealing to pair up Kittler with an even more famous analyst of bases and superstructures that he seems to be completely removed from: Karl Marx. Kittler – a thinker with limited sympathies on (and for) the political left – has on occasion spoken with high regard of Marx, though, in violation of the intellectual mainstream, he reserves his accolades for the older, "economistic" Marx of *Das Kapital* while showing little interest in the young, "humanist" Marx of the Parisian manuscripts. This is not surprising in light of the fact that the charges of technodeterminism raised against Kittler recall those against the economic determinism of Marx/Engels. It is worth recalling the famous letter Engels wrote to Joseph Bloch in September 1890 that dealt with this very accusation:

> According to the materialist conception of history, the ultimately determining element in history is the production and reproduction of real life. Other than this neither Marx nor I have ever asserted anything else. Hence if somebody twists this into saying that the economic element is the only determining one, he transforms that proposition into a meaningless, abstract, senseless phrase. (Marx and Engels 1975: 396)

Change two words and the diagnosis fits Kittler: the ultimately determining element is the production and reproduction of data, but to twist that into saying that the media-technological element is the only determining one is to transform the proposition into meaningless – or, at best, pretty trivial – insight. It is, of course, correct to say that for Kittler media technologies and cultural techniques are formative elements in the construction of differing discourse networks, but that is such a general assumption that it carries light analytical weight. But, as mentioned at the outset, Kittler no doubt is a guilty party. The desire to provoke, to replace the "human sauce of the Humanities in the 60s" (Kittler and Maresch 1994: 96) with a more rigid, external framework entailed exaggerations and provocations that could not but attract equally one-sided accusations. It also spawned contributions by younger scholars who are at times far more determinist than Kittler ever was. Engels, incidentally, admitted as much:

> Marx and I are ourselves partly to blame for the fact that the younger people sometimes lay more stress on the economic side than is due to it. We had to emphasize the main principle *vis-à-vis* our adversaries, who denied it, and we had not always the time, the place or the opportunity to give their due to the other elements involved in the interaction. (Marx and Engels 1975: 396)

2. WRITING (AND) WOMEN

Apart from technodetermism, the three most controversial areas of Kittler are the troublesome Ws: war, women, and writing style.

To begin with the last item: Kittler has been criticized, mocked, and condemned for his stylistic idiosyncrasies – all the more so because he has exerted considerable influence on a host of younger scholars. To connoisseurs of German academese (a pursuit with a certain entertainment value), so-called "Kittler German" or *Kittlerdeutsch* is as identifiable a linguistic subspecies as the more famous *Adornodeutsch* or *Heideggerdeutsch*. Among the most revealing lexical and syntactic features are, first, the inflationary use of adverbs like "simply," "merely," or "self-evidently" that denote simplicity precisely when things are not simple, and, second, a preference for turning subordinate relative clauses that begin with *weswegen*, *weshalb*, or *woraufhin* ("which is why," "wherefore," and "whereupon") into truncated main clauses. The former is a direct expression of Kittler's proclivity for clear text, that is, for pinpointing the basic or "simple" codes, algorithms, or structures underlying cultural production, while the latter tends to occur when he is out to make an important point. Which is why all sentences that begin with "which is why" simply deserve special attention.

Robert Holub has provided a comprehensive checklist of Kittler's rhetorical transgressions:

> Too often his arguments seem obscure and private. One frequently has the impression that the author is writing not to communicate, but to amuse himself. His text consists of a tapestry of leitmotifs, puns, and cryptic pronouncements, which at times makes for fascinating reading, but too often resembles free association as much as it does serious scholarship. As in much poststructuralist writing here and abroad, the often-cited rigor is more an assertion of the convinced than a fact of the prose: analysis frequently cedes to apodictic statement; logic repeatedly yields to rhetorical flourishes. (1992: 103–4)

This is an accurate summary (not to mention rather polite in comparison to what others have written) that contains the most conspicuous objectionable features. In line with the basic underlying thrust of his intellectual endeavor, the alternation between rapture and rule analysis, Kittler's texts swerve in vertiginous fashion between ellipsis and explicitness. Many things, especially theoretical presuppositions derived from so-called French theory, remain unexplained while others, in particular arcane technological details, are spelled out in great detail. Cryptic allusions, no doubt indebted to the esoteric ruminations of Lacan, give way to exhaustive manuals. At their best, Kittler's texts recall the hypothermal precision of Foucault's (though with a dash of bohemian humor that, surprisingly, appears to have been more widespread in Freiburg than in Paris); at their worst, they devolve into a wayward mix of theory-speak and technobabble.

Kittler's treatment of women presents a much thornier issue, which is particularly apparent in the first half of *Discourse Networks*. To repeat the core point of the analysis, the so-called age of Goethe excluded women from the inner circuits of literary production and relegated them either to the input position (as the inspiring, frequently eroticized sources of languages) or the output position (as female readers who in groupie-like fashion flock around male authors). Women read men in order to learn what it means to be women, mothers, or muses who teach or inspire men to speak. With the coming of the Discourse Network 1900, women enter the sexually closed circuits of the bygone era and become part of cultural production as secretaries and human typewriters, able to record the data streams emanating from men's mouths. Because women are now admitted to the inner circuits of the cultural wiring, Kittler's narrative tends to present this as an epochal shift that appears to involve a kind of promotion. Not surprisingly, female readers have raised the justified, ironically pointed question whether "the ability or the permission to take dictations was really so seminal" (Kloock and Spahr 1997: 17), that is, whether it is indeed so much better than what came before. Matters are exacerbated by Kittler's cavalier disdain for historical realities. When he in patronizing fashion concedes that nothing hindered women in the Discourse Network 1800 "from taking up the pen from time to time" (1990: 125), then this ignores the fact that the number of women writing and publishing between 1770 and 1830 was much higher than the flippant phrase "from time to time" indicates. But the crucial point is less the quantity of women writing than the question of how this can be reconciled with Kittler's basic analysis. Given the gender and language differentiations of the Discourse Network 1800 that originated at the cradle, how could women write? What relationship did girls have to the language of the mother? What is female writing in a world in which literary discourse is coded as exclusively male? How were so many women (whether or not they used male pseudonyms) able to occupy positions exclusively reserved for men?

To be sure, nobody has ever labeled Kittler a feminist or a gender theorist and probably nobody ever will. With sneering asides that describe "the literature of women, who write about nothing else than the fact they have become authors," as "trivial and *kalter Kaffee*" ("cold coffee" – the more dismissive German equivalent of English "old hat"), Kittler is unlikely to win any award for progressive male critic of the year (Kittler and Banz 1996: 48). And yet, surprisingly, in hindsight *Discourse Networks* represents one of the earliest and most ambitious German contributions to a historical analysis of gender construction. Regarding questions of sex and gender, Kittler's position is reminiscent of that of his Parisian *maître* Lacan. In her concise account of what French "discourse theories" can and cannot do for feminist politics, Nancy Fraser maintains that whatever contributions

Lacan made by successfully challenging ingrained notions of biologism (women and men are determined by their bodies) were undone by his no less confining mixture of symbolism and psychologism (women and men are determined by their inscription into a phallocentric symbolic order). "The speaking subject introduced by Lacan is not the agent of discursive practices. It is simply an effect of the symbolic order conjoined to some repressed libidinal drive" (Fraser 1992: 185). No matter how promising his emphasis on the pivotal importance of discourse for defining man and woman, in the final analysis Lacan offered nothing more than an escape into a neighboring cell. The same applies to Kittler: biologism is overcome by symbolism, which once again amounts to exchanging one type of confinement for another. However, the younger Kittler appears to gesture toward a way out of Lacan's cage by emphasizing the contingent, historical nature of the psychologist regimes. But to tease or blast this out of *Discourse Networks* (as Wellbery tried to do in his introduction to the English translation) would have required a conceptual toolbox capable of combining Kittler's radically historical approach with the notion of discursive gender performativity. Such a toolbox was nowhere to be found in the mid-1980s in Germany. To put it bluntly, the problem with Kittler's analysis is that it appeared in the dark days before Judith Butler's books shook up German academia. Since there was little conceptual expertise available to tackle the gender question, it was easier to dismiss Kittler's discourse machismo out of hand. And by the time gender theory reached the point where it could have separated the useful wheat from the sexist chaff, Kittler himself had moved on, or rather back, into a naturalized heteronormative gender portrayal. In the Greek books women appear to be by nature what in the earlier book they were by discourse: intriguing, eroticized, and more often than not singing objects of desire that make men write, rhyme, and philosophize.

3. MICK JAGGER'S BLITZKRIEG AND THE MACHINE SUBJECTS

But all these debates pale in comparison to the issue of war. It is such a hot topic that it produced some of Kittler's most memorable gaffes:

> I am not one of those theorists who despise the German *Wehrmacht* and its military operations. There has, for example, been much talk recently of the brutality of the *Wehrmacht* in the Russian campaign during the Second World War and I understand that. Nonetheless, it is obvious [. . .] to me that the real riddle of the Second World War is how it was possible for Hitler's *Blitzkrieg* to conquer the whole of Europe, except Finland, in two years? This to me was an *incredible* event. (Armitage 2006: 27)

The whole of Europe? This may come as a surprise to Spanish, Portuguese, Irish, Scottish, English, Icelandic, Swedish, and Swiss readers; not to mention the fact that more than two years separated the initial blitzkrieg from the German occupation of many Eastern European countries. Given how meticulous (and unforgiving of others' mistakes) Kittler tends to be in techno-military matters, this massive blunder comes as a surprise. What relays were being (mis) switched in his mind to produce it?

The second gaffe – less conspicuous but ultimately more revealing – concerns the German computer pioneer Konrad Zuse (1910–95). Kittler claims that Zuse's Z4, a programmable, relay-based electronic data-processing machine, which despite the fact that it did not feature conditional jumps many consider the first Turing-complete computer (see Agar 2001: 41–52), was involved in "determining in the bunkers of the Harz the fate of the V2" (Kittler 1999: 259). That is to say, the Z4 was allegedly used to program the flight paths of V2 rockets aimed at Britain. Factually, this is wrong. Kittler could easily have avoided the gaffe if he had done what he normally does very well: namely, read – in this case, the pertinent parts of Zuse's memoirs. Zuse recounts a picaresque, if not pynchonesque, story. The Z4, the fourth machine assembled in his parents' apartment in Berlin, was also known as the V4. The "V" stands for *Versuchsmodell* ("experimental model"), and because this looked a lot like V2 (which, to add to the confusion, was also known as the A4), one of his collaborators managed to persuade the authorities to order Zuse and his fellow workers to evacuate the Z4/V4 from the approaching Red Army to one of the underground ordnance factories in Thuringia where thousands of concentration camp inmates were assembling the V2/A4 rockets. The group took one look at the inhuman conditions and escaped to the South German Allgäu region to sit out the end of the war (see Zuse 1993: 91–4). To a certain extent Kittler is excused; he merely quoted an otherwise impeccable source, Andrew Hodges's excellent biography of Alan Turing, which claims that "Zuse calculators were used in the engineering of V2 rockets, and in 1945 Zuse himself was installed in the Dora underground factories" (Hodges 1983: 299). Hodges has since acknowledged the mistake. But there is more to Kittler's mistake. It was a case of wishful thinking, and ultimately the desire in question is directly related to Kittler's view of war, in particular, of World War II.

Between the mid-1980s and the turn of the millennium, it was almost impossible to tackle any of his texts without coming across passages that highlight the central importance of modern war for the evolution of media. War appears as the father of all things technical; the medial a priori collapses into a martial a priori. *Gramophone, Film, Typewriter* is the most explicit text. The 1-3-1 narrative (writing-differentiation into analog media-digital sublation) is said to be caused by a succession of wars:

> Phase 1, beginning with the American Civil War, developed storage technologies for acoustics, optics, and script: film, gramophone, and the man-machine system, typewriter. Phase 2, beginning with the First World War, developed for each storage content appropriate electric transmission technologies: radio, television, and their more secret counterparts. Phase 3, since the Second World War, has transferred the schematic of a typewriter of predictability per se; Turing's mathematical definition of computability in 1936 gave future computers their name. (Kittler 1999: 243)

The war to end all wars leads to the medium to end all media. "The unwritten history of technical norms is a history of war" (Kittler 1998b: 56). All the fancy entertainment gadgets that distract us between wars are nothing but weapons technologies in disguise. Whether it is a matter of hi-fi technology living off innovations in aircraft and submarine location technologies, or of radio stations exploiting the VHF frequency modulation and signal multiplexing that had been indispensable for the successful coordination of "incredible" *Wehrmacht* panzer tactics, "[t]he entertainment industry" – to quote one of Kittler's most (in)famous aperçus – "is, in any conceivable sense of the word, nothing but an abuse of army equipment" (1999: 96–7). And sometimes you just need to listen in order to hear the martial truth. Take, for instance, the lyrics from the Rolling Stones' "Sympathy with the Devil": "I rode a tank / held a gen'rals's rank / when the blitzkrieg raged / and the bodies stank." The finest hour for discourse analysis came when Kittler had Mick Jagger implode into Colonel General Guderian, one of the principal architects of modern blitzkrieg. Much as Goethe's "Wanderer's Nightsong" is referred straight back to the maternal *ur*-scene of the Discourse Network 1800's new matricentric language acquisition practices, Kittler collapses "Sympathy with the Devil" into the war-propeled development of VHF radio that enabled the coordination of Guderian's panzer tactics, and, subsequently, rock music's guidance of motorized "tourist divisions, which under so-called postwar conditions rehearse or simulate the blitzkrieg" (1999: 108).

Though the entertainment industry may strive to conceal the military origins of their media, these are so suffused with war that it remains their inescapable horizon. While soldiers fight the last war, media are preparing the next: "VHF tank radio, vocoders, Magnetophones, submarine location technologies, air war radio beams, etc., have released an abuse of army equipment that adapts ears and reaction speeds to World War *n+1*. Radio, the first abuse, led from World War I to World War II, rock music, the next abuse, from II to III" (1999: 111). Not only is the history of media and information technology the history of war in a nutshell and "[t]he unwritten history of technical norms a history of war" (1998b: 56), but the sensory drill imposed upon us by weapons systems posing as entertainment gadgets amounts to an ongoing collective neurophysiological boot camp, designed to bring us up to the reaction speeds of the next electronic war. Which, incidentally, is necessary because humans are too slow for fast wars:

In terms of motor skills, sensory perception and intellectual acumen, people are evidently not designed to wage

Hi-tech wars. Ever since the First World War [. . .] speed and acceleration have mandated the creation of special training camps that teach new forms of perception to sluggish people and accustom them to man-machine-synergies. This started in 1914 with the wristwatch and it will not end with today's combat simulators. We can assume that in the interim period, when wars are not running in real-time, rock concerts and discos function as boot camps for perceptions that undermine the thresholds of perception. (Kittler 1993a: 90).

You can take the media out of war, but you can never take the war out of media. "Our discos are preparing our youth for a retaliatory strike" (Kittler 1999: 140).

To be sure, countless objections are lining up and shuffling their feet. The military origins of many modern media technologies are beyond doubt, but there are also cases in which war and/or the military disregarded, at times even obstructed, new media. The telephone, a technology of predominantly civilian provenance, had obvious potential for securing communications on the modern battlefield, yet the German army (one of the key players in Kittler's grand martial narrative) initially resisted its adoption out of fear that it would erode military discipline (see Kaufmann 1996: 189–219). Subordinates receiving orders over the phone may be tempted to no longer click their heels. Forty years later, the German army snubbed its nose at Zuse's offer to use his early computer as an encryption machine instead of the allegedly spy-proof Enigma. Had the *Wehrmacht* acted more in line with Kittler's high regard of it, Alan Turing and Bletchley Park would not have been able to crack the German code.

The problem, however, goes far beyond factual blunders. To begin with there is a noticeable fuzziness or, to stick to martial metaphors, a set of artfully deployed smoke screens that shield Kittler from enemy fire. First, it is not quite clear whether war is instrumentally involved in the production or in the diffusion of modern media technology. On the one hand, Kittler claims that "media were developed for technological wars" (1993a: 102), hence wars are "in truth and fact the historical apriori" (2003a: 56) of modern media. On the other hand, he provides a detailed overview of the very unmilitary genesis of radio technology, only to add: "A world war, the first of its kind, had to break out to facilitate the switch from Poulsen's arc transmission to Lieben or De Forest's tube-type technology and the mass production of Fessenden's experimental procedure" (1999: 95). In response, critics have raised the ironic question of whether this means "that without WWI radio technology would have been gathering dust in the basement[s] of various universities" (Goldstrasz and Panthle 2010). More importantly, the meaning of the term "war" shifts. At times it refers, literally and profanely, to military confrontations, but sometimes it connotes a great deal more. "War, as opposed to sheer fighting, has been for a long time an affair of persuasion. It came into being only when people succeeded in making others die for them" (Kittler 1997: 117). In short, war frequently refers to what is commonly known as *mobilization*.

Mobilization erodes the boundaries between war and peace because it takes place in both; it erodes the boundary between the military and the civilian population because it affects one as much as the other; and it erodes the distinction between material hardware and psychic software because it deals as much with the optimization of logistics, transport, and technology as with increasing mental preparedness and overall combat readiness. But what kind of human is most equipped (or least under-equipped) to deal with the acceleration and incomprehensibility of modern war? What type of mind is able to make rapid, on-the-spot decisions, or even make up new rules when no flag, no commanding authority, is in sight? What has been programmed to fight with a free will? The modern *subject*.

In his afterword to the German edition of the works of Alan Turing (which he co-edited), Kittler cites a top-ranking German philosopher whom he normally avoids and with whom (unlike Hegel, Nietzsche, Heidegger) he has very little in common: Immanuel Kant. The following quote from the *Anthropology from a Pragmatic Point of View* is an attempt to illustrate the – for Kant – pivotal difference between *Verstand* (understanding), *Urteilskraft* (judgment) and *Vernunft* (reason):

> The domestic or civil servant, who is acting under orders, requires no more than understanding; the officer, who in order to complete a task has only been provided with a general rule and who is left to decide on his own what to do in a specific case, is in need of judgment; the general, who has to judge all possible cases and think up a rule on his own, must possess reason. (Kant, quoted in Kittler 1987: 223)

Kittler reads this quote just as he had read Freud's telephonic illustration of the unconscious. He takes literally what Kant inserted as helpful comparisons: generals are not just like subjects; they are their prototypes. The ascending hierarchy of understanding, the judgment around which Kantian epistemology revolves, is a military chain of command because the new forms of enlightened consciousness are products of the attempts to turn feudal and absolutist automatons into self-directed agents. The mental faculties we need in order to perform our civic duties, in the Kafkaesque quagmire of a decentered, functionally differentiated modern society that no longer provides any all-encompassing rules and guidelines, are precisely what we need in order to perform our military duties on the decentered modern battlefield. Modern subjects are soldiers that have learned to think on their own. The whole narrative of literacy, soulfulness, and Romantic hermeneutics detailed in the first part of *Discourse Networks* can be recast in a martial vein. The history of reason belongs to the history of war.

To top it off, the fact that modern subjects are self-directed agents capable of recursive reflection – that is, of reacting to unforeseen circumstances by rewriting the initial set of instructions – allows them to be replaced by modern weapons. As Kittler would have it, our philosophically embellished features of self-reflexivity are just as present in *non-trivial machine subjects*. Bluntly put, there is not much difference between a self-directed human and a self-directed cruise missile. Kittler introduces this equivalence with a Lacanian spin by emphasizing that the crucial feature that turns mere machines into machine subjects is the implementation of conditional jump instructions or IF/THEN-commands. Quoting Lacan, Kittler insists that the difference between a straightforward mechanical command that determines exactly how an operation should be executed from beginning to end (which in Kant's illustration is the level of the simple servant or soldier), and a program that enables the operator to alter its behavior during the operation once or if certain conditions have been met (Kant's officer), is the same as the distinction between an animal code and a language involving human subjectivity:

> For example, the dance of bees, as is has been researched by von Frisch, "is distinguished from language precisely by the fixed correlation of its signs to the reality they signify." While the messages of one bee control the flight of another to blossoms and prey, these messages are not decoded and transmitted by the second bee. By contrast, "the form in

which language is expressed [. . .] itself defines subjectivity. Language says: 'You will go here, and when you see this, you will turn off there.' In other words, it refers itself to the discourse of the other." In yet other words: bees are projectiles, and humans, cruise missiles. One is given objective data on angles and distances by a dance, the other, a command of free will. (Kittler 1999: 258–9)

Subjective agency is conceived of as operational reflexivity which, translated into the computational realm, takes on the shape of feedback commands. This allows Kittler to establish a functional equivalence between human operators and cruise missiles as machine subjects, and to claim that the latter have ousted the former since they are able to receive, process, and execute incoming information in superior fashion. Once again, this does not mean that computers are artificial human brains, or that they digitally ape specifically human ways of thinking. Rather, they optimize certain patterns of information processing that were also imposed on human beings but subsequently were mistaken to be innately human qualities. Subjects emerge from war only to be replaced by more efficient machine subjects.

4. WHY WAR? FROM PEENEMÜNDE TO PYNCHON

War is such a central and controversial issue in Kittler's work that the attempt to explain its high profile goes a long way toward providing a central assessment of Kittler's entire oeuvre. So, why is war so important? Because for the more martially inclined Kittler of the 1980s and 1990s war is *motor*, *model*, and *motive*.

The notion that war drives media history has less to do with questionable historical evidence than with a basic quandary related to Kittler's update of Foucault. To briefly repeat, Kittler grounded several of Foucault's discursive irruptions in media-technological shifts. The advent of analog media, for instance, put an end to Foucault's "modern" period (which corresponds to Kittler's Discourse Network 1800). The basic message is that epistemes change because media change. But this is not much of an answer since it begs the obvious question: why do media change? Given Kittler's reticence to attribute any kind of technological evolution to socio-economic factors, war (which in Kittler's world is not much of a social event) provides a convenient answer: media shifts are due to military exigencies. World War II – to be precise, the need to decrypt intercepted German messages – was the motor that drove that evolution of the computer, thus initiating the switch from the analog Discourse Network 1900 to the digital age. In short, war is the *explanans*, the fundamental reason why media and discursive regimes change.

But, once again, things start to get fuzzy. Have a look at this revealing passage from the introductory section of *Optical Media*:

> [W]hen the development of a media subsystem is analyzed in all of its historical breadth [. . .], the [. . .] suspicion arises that technical innovations – following the model of military escalations – only refer to and answer to each other, and the end result of this proprietary development, which progresses completely independent of individual or even collective bodies of people, is an overwhelming impact on senses and organs in general. (2010: 30)

Note how in this passage "military escalation" is qualified as a model. The intermedial dynamics that shape and reshape societies are not driven by war; they are *like* war. This is another instance of the superimposition that marks the bellicose portions of Kittler's writings. Sometimes war is "in truth and fact" the agent behind all technological change; sometimes it is a mere model or metaphor. War is both *explanans* and *illustrans*; it explains media-historical change and it supplies a provocative metaphor directly aimed at all social theories that privilege human progress, enlightenment, communication, and reconciliation over the fundamentally adversarial nature of human–machine and machine–machine interaction.

However, we need to add one caveat: once you accept the premise that from a certain point on technological evolution departs from human evolution because technologies are designing and producing their next generations without the need for human intermediaries, the constant shift from motor to model and back loses some of its irritating fuzziness. If technology in the broadest sense of the word (i.e., including sign systems and cultural techniques and practices) *is* history, then the internal dynamics of an autonomous technological evolution are both the driving force and the shape of all the secondary social dynamics that are impacted by it. In much the same way as Hegel's philosophy positions conflict in the very center of history because the ongoing process of diremption and struggle is central to the way in which the Absolute Spirit meanders toward self-realization, Kittler's account merges war and the progress of technology by basing the latter on constant competition and one-upmanship. Here, students of media theory will once again notice the proximity to Innis. Innis's account of how the rule of papyrus created conditions for its supersession by parchment, which, in turn, was overcome by paper, is remarkably similar to Kittler's war-inflected narrative of how the mechanical semaphore, which outdid messengers on horseback, gave rise to and was ousted by electric cables, which themselves were overcome by wireless technologies that, in turn, gave rise to digital decoding technologies (see Kittler 2003a: 262). In both cases, media and communication technologies evolve by strategic escalation, though Kittler attempts to make the struggle more concrete by tying it to actual military conflicts. At times Kittler reads like Innis dressed in combat fatigues.

Finally, we need to address the slippery – and extra-theoretical – question of motive. As pointed out in the biographical chapter 1, Kittler grew up in an environment in which World War II was both eerily present and suppressed, an uncanny situation that was particularly noticeable during childhood trips to the Baltic Sea, close to the former military proving ground of Peenemünde:

> From early childhood my mother often took me to the site in East Germany where Hitler's V2 rockets were developed during the Second World War. However, what fascinated me most about these sites and rockets was the fact that no one said a word about them. And yet the traces [. . .] were everywhere. And so I had to find my own explanation for this hidden part of history. But it was difficult to do because it was almost forbidden to talk about the military-indus-trial complex in East Germany or even to speak about the German side of the war effort more generally, and espe-cially anything that touched on the technological side of the war. (Armitage 2006: 25–6).

Kittler relates that he did not grasp the importance of Peenemünde until he came across *Gravity's Rainbow*, which impacted him like "a positive shockwave" and "lifted a kind of dark veil from my eyes concerning my own childhood experiences with V2s" (Armitage 2006: 26). For Kittler, Pynchon's novel presented a view of the war conspicuously absent from the history books and political punditry he had grown up with:

> [T]his war was never political at all, the politics was all theatre, all just to keep the people distracted . . . secretly, it was being dictated instead by the needs of technology . . . by a conspiracy between human beings and techniques, by something that needed the energy-burst of war, crying, "Money be damned, the very life of [insert name of Nation] is at stake," but meaning, most likely, dawn is nearly here, I need my night's blood, my funding, funding, ahh more, more. . . . The real crises were crises of allocation and priority, not among firms – it was only staged to look that way – but among the different Technologies, Plastics, Electronics, Aircraft, and their needs which are understood only by the ruling elite. (Pynchon 1987: 521)

This World War II has little to do with politics and ideology, it is not about living spaces for master races or grand crusades to liberate Europe. Whatever the many human players may be doing or dreaming of in Pynchon's novel, they are no more than minor appendages in a story that culminates on a very different, trans-human scale. Backed by Pynchon's novel, Kittler can present World War II as a crucial episode in the most momentous boy-meets-girl story of the twentieth century, the industrial-scale link-up between German rocket and Anglo-American computer technology (see Kittler 1997: 101–16). History completes itself (for the time being) as a fully armored, self-guiding Owl of Minerva touches down in Peenemünde, Bletchley Park, and, ultimately, Los Alamos. And this explains the wishful thinking behind Kittler's Z4/A4-gaffe: If Zuse's early computer had been used to program Wernher von Braun's V2, the momentous technological synthesis would have been, at least initially, a thoroughly German affair.

For a long time, then, one of the principal motives driving Kittler's work was the desire to make sense of what he considers to be the real meaning of modern wars, and of World War II in particular – for himself, for Germany, and for our global technological realities. There is more than a passing resemblance to another highly controversial author revered by Kittler, Ernst Jünger (1895–1998), whose essays "Total Mobilization" (Jünger 1992), *On Pain* (Jünger 2008), and the as yet untranslated *Der Arbeiter* ("The Worker") similarly attempt to process the impact of the technological dimensions of World War I at the expense of the usual political and ideological accounts. Eschewing the latter, both Kittler and Jünger end up in the rarefied realm of a technological super-evolution that at times takes on an almost mythical hue. Yet the reference to the – at least in the 1920s – extremely right-wing Jünger with his polemic disdain for conventional humanism points toward Kittler's controversial stance: there is no Hitler in Kittler's war, no war of aggression, no final solution, no complicity of military conquest and racial genocide, and subsequently no question of guilt and responsibility. Just as French theorists like Foucault and Lacan enabled Kittler to deal with Heidegger in an updated and roundabout way when it was not opportune to be caught standing on his shoulders, an American novel allowed Kittler to focus on the decisive techno-military features of World War II while avoiding what he dismisses as the "Auschwitz-theoretical" (Kittler and Banz 1996: 9) aspects. Whether this would meet with Pynchon's approval is doubtful; ironically, Pynchon's novels *V* and *Gravity's Rainbow* have done their share to expand awareness of the genocidal dimension of German history by drawing connections between the Nazi Holocaust and the annihilation of the Hereros by the German army in 1904. And with regard to the Zuse gaffe: what is left unsaid by Kittler is that the all-German link-up would have taken place in the Mittelbau-Dora concentration camp, one of the most brutal labor camps ever created by the SS.

5. FINAL CHECKLIST: THE KITTLER EFFECT

Is there a "Kittler School"? Yes, but it is not worth talking about. As in the case of Heidegger, clones can be dismissed, for those who choose to think and write like Kittler are condemned to forever repeat him. However, the contributions of a fair number of German media scholars and cultural theorists are influenced by Kittler, although they have gone beyond (and occasionally against) the master to produce outstanding work in their own right. This does not make them "Kittlerians" (as little as Kittler himself is a Foucauldian), but it is fair to say that their encounter with Kittler was as important to them as the encounter with Foucault was for him. Assessing indebtedness to Kittler is in any case a difficult task. It is not easy to sit on the shoulders of someone whose preferred gesture is to shrug things off.

It makes more sense to speak of a "Kittler effect," meaning, in the simplest possible terms, that Kittler has set certain benchmarks that are difficult to ignore, no matter how much you may disagree with the details. The net result is not so much the introduction of something completely new that was not there before, but rather the rapid aging of much that was already there. After Kittler, a lot seems outdated. It is extremely difficult to summarize his – at times very ambiguous – achievements, even if we restrict ourselves to those of particular importance to students of media and communication, but in the final analysis it boils down to three points.

1. Regardless of factual inaccuracies and methodological inconsistencies, Kittler provides one of the most effective antidotes against the presentism and uniformitarianism that

are especially pervasive in North American communication studies. Kittler is a radically historical thinker. The concept of discourse networks is not only indebted to Heidegger and Foucault, but is also a radicalization of nineteenth-century German historicism. In ways which were not there before, Kittler introduced the idea of fundamental discontinuity to media studies; and, while he may go over the top at times, his radicalism may serve as a safeguard against the naive temporal extrapolations that are all too common in the discipline. The second aspect is the sheer scope of the enterprise. Not since Innis has there been an attempt to model changes of the medial and communicational structures on such a historical scale – an expansion that is especially recommended to countries obsessed with modernism and its aftermath.

2. Regardless of Kittler's complex relationship to, and eventual demotion of, poststructuralism (and regardless of the validity of the term), Kittler's work has established a benchmark when it comes to negotiating between "French theory," from Lacan to Virilio and the increased academic focus on media-technological issues. By importing so-called poststructuralist theory (whether inspired by Heidegger or not) to media studies, Kittler has been instrumental in removing a long-standing naivety from the discussion of technology. By bringing an informed media-technological perspective to French theory (and its German precursors), he has grounded thinkers like Lacan, Foucault, and Derrida in technological realities that they themselves were at times only able to process on a metaphorical and anecdotal level. "French theory" (which was an American invention to begin with) will most likely never be the same; at the very least it will no longer be French.

3. Regardless of the marked differences between Kittler, on the one hand, and Innis and McLuhan, on the other, it makes sense to establish a certain proximity between them,

especially in light of the respective national discourses on media that inform their work (see also Winthrop-Young 2006a, 2008). McLuhanites may resent the patronizing implications, but Kittler has been instrumental in restoring a certain informed respectability to issues tarnished by McLuhan's unchecked loquaciousness. In particular, it is difficult to ignore the fact that Kittler's contributions have provided a revised framework for the discussion of media determinism, including the discussion whether he himself falls under that category. And for the ongoing discussions of posthumanism, Kittler's anti-humanism may turn out to be one of the most important contributions when it comes to the question of human-machine co-evolution.

John Peters, one of the few North American media theorists with a thorough knowledge of Kittler's work, concludes his introduction to the translation of Kittler's *Optical Media* with an interesting eulogy:

> In the end, what I like best about Kittler is his sheer love of intelligence and his commitment to delirious delight as a path to higher wisdom. Like all of us, Friedrich Kittler can be blind, but like very few of us, he can also be absolutely dazzling. (Peters 2010: 16)

Much like William Blake, who lurks in the background of this praise, Kittler is a singular – some would say, singularly erratic – figure (Blake has many admirers but few followers). But if the fate of past radicals, especially those marked by an intriguing backward-looking up-to-dateness, holds any clues, Kittler will suffer the usual cruel fate reserved for rebellious classics: integration. What started out as an uncompromising alternative to the academic mainstream will be incorporated in the shape of simple readjustments. The battle cry "media determine our situation" is reduced to the tacit agreement that scholars should pay some attention to media formats after having paid none at all for decades. What Kittler wrote about the changing language acquisition practices in the late eighteenth century will survive as a footnote in future histories of the genesis of the bourgeois intimacy. The discourse analysis of the civil servant state will be acknowledged as an interesting gloss on the well-known narrative that German literature and philosophy emerged from a rarefied cast of academics and civil servants rather than from a vigorous class of entrepreneurs. Exaggerations and provocations will be defused and incorporated by measured compromises. But once the latter start to rot, the time will be ripe for new provocations. Kittler will deliver them.

FURTHER READING

The following information is intended for interested readers with little or no knowledge of Kittler (and little or no knowledge of German). Almost all the recommended texts are in English.

A. Principal works in English

Three books (Kittler 1990, 1999, 2010) and one collection (Kittler 1997) have so far been published in English. The most accessible book is the lecture on *Optical Media* (Kittler 2010). The section on "Theoretical Presuppositions" (29–46) is the most straightforward account written by Kittler himself on some of his basic methodological and theoretical premises. As the title indicates, the text only deals with optical media. Kittler's greatest strength, however, lies with acoustic media, which receive their most concise treatment in the "Gramophone" section of *Gramophone, Film, Typewriter* (1999: 21–114). For those interested in Kittler's work on digital technology, *Literature Media Information*

Systems, an excellent collection edited by John Johnston, contains the provocative hardware/software essays "There is No Software" (Kittler 1997: 147–68) and "Protected Mode" (ibid.: 156–68). It also features the famous "Dracula" essay (ibid.: 50–84), though readers are forewarned that they will have to wade through a number of cryptic Lacanian digressions. *Discourse Networks* (Kittler 1990), the "damned learned book" (Kittler and Weinberger 2009: 94), is not for the fainthearted; especially the first part on the Discourse Network 1800, which presupposes a certain familiarity with German literature and philosophy of the so-called age of Goethe.

In addition to the book-length texts several essays have been published, of which three are of particular importance: "Thinking Colours and/or Machines" (Kittler 2006c), "Towards an Ontology of Media" (Kittler 2009), and "History of Communication Media" (available online at: <http://www.ctheory.net/articles.aspx?id=45>). All three are historical overviews; while the first two focus on the uneasy relationship between philosophy and media(lity), the third presents Kittler's bird's-eye view of the overall evolution of communication and storage media.

B. Introductions and overviews

Kittler's translated books come with introductions (Johnston 1997; Peters 2010; Wellbery 1990; Winthrop-Young and Wutz 1999), all of which should be read before or while tackling the texts. David Wellbery's preface to *Discourse Networks* (Kittler 1990: vii–xxxiii) is arguably the single most informative piece in English on Kittler's theoretical presuppositions. Much like Johnston's introduction to *Literature Media Information Systems* (Kittler 1997: 2–26), it is aimed at positioning Kittler within the North American theory debates, while the introduction by Geoffrey Winthrop-Young and Michael Wutz to *Gramophone, Film, Typewriter*

(Kittler 1999: xi–xxxvii) is geared toward situating Kittler in a German context. Those interested in a quick overview should read either the Kittler chapter in *Digital Matters* (Taylor and Harris 2005: 66–86) or the introductory essay for the *Theory, Culture & Society* special on Kittler (Winthrop-Young and Gane 2006).

C. Specialized contributions

There is a growing number of essays on particular aspects of Kittler's work, of which the following five are of particular interest. Holub (1992: 97–107) provides a highly critical, but very informed, account of Kittler's early work that should be read alongside Wellbery's more positive introduction to *Discourse Networks*. Sybille Krämer's paper on time-axis manipulation is as indispensable for understanding Kittler's take on analog storage technology (Krämer 2006) as Claudia Breger's essay, "Gods, German Scholars and the Gift of Greece," is for understanding the (national) cultural context of Kittler's Greek work (Breger 2006). John Peters's "Strange Sympathies" (Peters 2008) offers an intriguing comparison between Kittler and the American communication theorist James Carey, and Winthrop-Young's "Drill and Distraction in the Yellow Submarine" (Winthrop-Young 2002) offers a more extensive account of Kittler's martial bent than was possible here.

D. Interviews and online lectures

Kittler tends to be a no-holds-barred interviewee, as can be glimpsed from John Armitage's very revealing, occasionally slightly embarrassing, and therefore highly recommended interview "Cultural Mathematics" (Armitage 2006). Less scandalous, but equally informative, is the 1996 interview conducted by Matthew Griffith and Susanne Herrmann (Griffith and Herrmann 1996). For a combination of matters

Greek and post-digital, see the co-interview with Mark Hansen (Gane and Sale 2007). Some of Kittler's lectures are online, though most of them are delivered in German. One exception is "The Relation of Art and Techne," given at European Graduate School in 2005 (<http://www.egs.edu/faculty/friedrich-kittler/videos/the-relation-of-art-and-techne/>).

E. Bibliographic resources
The most extensive bibliography of Kittler's works up until 2002 is in the (German) Festschrift published on the occasion of his sixtieth birthday (Berz, Bitsch, and Siegert 2003: 359–74). Students may also wish to consult the periodically updated online bibliography at <http://hydra.humanities.uci.edu/kittler/kittlerpub.html>.

WORKS CITED

Agar, J., 2001. *Turing and the Universal Machine: The Making of the Modern Computer*. Duxford: Icon Books.

Aly, G., 2008. *Unser Kampf: 1968 – ein irritierter Blick zurück*. Frankfurt: Fischer.

Arata, S., 1990. The Occidental Tourist: Dracula and the Anxiety of Reverse Colonization. *Victorian Studies* 33: 621–45.

Armitage, J., 2006. From Discourse Networks to Cultural Mathematics: An Interview with Friedrich A. Kittler. *Theory, Culture & Society* 23(7–8): 17–38.

Assmann, A., and J. Assmann, 1990. Einleitung. In E. Havelock, *Schriftlichkeit: Das griechische Alphabet als kulturelle Revolution*. Weinheim: VCH, pp. 1–35.

Bambach, C., 2005. *Heidegger's Roots: Nietzsche, National Socialism and the Greeks*. Ithaca, NY: Cornell University Press.

Benjamin, W., 1969. *Illuminations: Essays and Reflections*. Ed. Hannah Arendt. New York: Schocken.

Benn, G., 1984. *Gesammelte Werke in der Fassung der Erstdrucke*. Ed. B. Hillebrand. Frankfurt: Fischer.

Berz, P., A. Bitsch, and B. Siegert, eds, 2003. *FAKtisch. Festschrift für Friedrich Kittler*. Munich: Fink.

Bolz, N., 1990. *Theorie der neuen Medien*. Munich: Raben.

Boyle. N., 2008. *German Literature: A Very Short Introduction*. Oxford: Oxford University Press.

Breger, C., 2006. Gods, German Scholars and the Gift of Greece: Friedrich Kittler's Philhellenic Fantasies. *Theory, Culture & Society* 23(7–8): 111–34.

Burkert, W., 1992. *The Orientalizing Revolution: Near Eastern Influence on Greek Culture in the Early Archaic Age*. Cambridge, MA: Harvard University Press.

Butler, E. M., 1935. *The Tyranny of Greece over Germany: A Study of the Influence Exercised by Greek Art and Poetry over the Great German Writers of the Eighteenth, Nineteenth and Twentieth Centuries*. Cambridge: Cambridge University Press.

Carey, J., 1969. Harold Adams Innis and Marshall McLuhan. In R. Rosenthal, ed., *McLuhan: Pro & Con*. Baltimore, MD: Penguin, pp. 270–308.

Cunningham, M., 1997. Welcome to the Machine: The Story of Pink Floyd's Live Sound: PART 1, *Sound on Stage* 5 at: <www.pinkfloyd-co.com/band/interviews/art-rev/art-sos1.html> (accessed 1 June, 2010).

Cusset, F., 2008. *French Theory: How Foucault, Derrida, Deleuze, and Co. Transformed the Intellectual Life of the United States*. Trans. J. Fort. Minneapolis, MN: University of Minnesota Press.

Eliot. T. S., 2005. Tradition and the Individual Talent. In L. Rainey, ed., *Modernism: An Anthology*. Oxford: Blackwell, pp. 152–6.

Foucault, M., 1994. *The Order of Things: An Archaeology of the Human Sciences*. New York: Vintage.

Fraser, N., 1992. *The Uses and Abuses of French Discourse Theories for Feminist Politics.* In N. Fraser and S. L. Bartky, eds, *Revaluing French Feminism.* Bloomington, IN: Indiana University Press, pp. 177–93.

Freud, S., 1962. *The Standard Edition of the Complete Psychological Works of Sigmund Freud.* Ed. J. Strachey. London: Hogarth.

Gane, N., and S. Sale, 2007. Interview with Friedrich Kittler and Mark Hansen. *Theory, Culture and Society* 24(7–8), pp. 323–29.

Gelatt, R., 1977. *The Fabulous Phonograph, 1877–1977.* New York: Macmillan.

Goethe, J. W., 1978. *Werke: Hamburger Ausgabe in 14 Bänden.* Munich: Beck.

Goldstrasz, T., and Panthle, H. Computers During World War Two. Kittler's Theory of Misuse. Available at: <http://waste.informatik.hu-berlin.de/Diplom/WW2/kittlertheory.html> (accessed March 1, 2010).

Griffith, M., and S. Herrmann, 1996. Technologies of Writing: Interview with Friedrich Kittler. *New Literary History* 27 (4): 731–42.

Hagen. W., 2008. Metaxy: Eine historiosemantische Fussnote zum Medienbegriff. In S. Münker and A. Roesler, eds, *Was ist ein Medium?* Frankfurt: Suhrkamp, pp. 13–29.

Hartmann, F., 1998. Vom Sündenfall der Software: Medientheorie mit Entlarvungsgestus: Friedrich Kittler. Available at: <http://www.heise.de/tp/r4/artikel/6/6345/1.html> (accessed May 20, 2010).

Havelock, E., 1978. The Alphabetization of Homer. In E. Havelock and J. Hershbell, eds, *Communication Arts in the Ancient World.* New York: Hastings House, pp. 3–21.

Hegel, G. W. F., 1977. *Phenomenology of Spirit.* Trans. A. V. Miller. Oxford: Oxford University Press.

Heidegger, M., 1992. *Parmenides*. Trans. A. Schuwer and R. Rojcewicz. Bloomington, IN: Indiana University Press.

Heine, H., 2006. *The Romantic School and Other Essays*. Ed. Robert Holub. New York: Continuum.

Heller, A., 2008. The Gods of Greece: Germans and the Greeks. *Thesis Eleven* 93: 52–63.

Hodges, A., 1983. *Alan Turing: The Enigma*. New York: Simon and Schuster.

Hoffmann, E. T. A., 1969. *Selected Writings*. Ed. and trans. L. J. Kent and E. C. Knight. Chicago, IL: University of Chicago Press.

Holub, R., 1992. *Crossing Borders: Reception Theory, Poststructuralism, Deconstruction*. Madison, WI: University of Wisconsin Press.

Homer, 1991. *The Iliad*. Trans. R. Fagles. New York: Viking.

Homer, 1996. *The Odyssey*. Trans. R. Fagles. New York: Viking.

Horkheimer, M., and T. Adorno, 1972. *Dialectic of Enlightenment*. New York: Herder and Herder.

Johnston, J., 1997. Friedrich Kittler: Media Theory after Poststructuralism. In F. Kittler (1997), pp. 2–26.

Jones, C., 1996. *Echoes: The Stories behind Every Pink Floyd Song*. London: Carlton.

Jünger, E., 1992. Total Mobilization. In R. Wolin, ed., *The Heidegger Controversy*. Cambridge, MA: MIT Press, pp. 119–29.

Jünger, E., 2008. *On Pain*. Trans. David. C. Durst. New York: Telus.

Kant. I., 1949. *The Philosophy of Kant: Immanuel Kant's Moral and Political Writings*. New York: Modern Library.

Kaufmann, S., 1996. *Kommunikationstechnik und Kriegsführung 1815–1945*. Munich: Fink.

Kittler, F., 1977. *Der Traum und die Rede: Eine Analyse der*

Kommunikationssituation Conrad Ferdinand Meyers. Bern: Francke.

Kittler, F., 1980. Autorschaft und Liebe. In F. Kittler, ed., *Austreibung des Geistes aus den Geisteswissenschaften. Programme des Poststrukturalismus*. Paderborn: Schöningh, pp. 142–73.

Kittler, F., 1982. England 1975 – Pink Floyd, Brain Damage. In K. Lindemann, ed., *Europalyrik 1775-heute. Gedichte und Interpretationen*. Paderborn: Schöningh, pp. 467–77.

Kittler. F., 1985. Ein Verwaiser. In Gesa Dane et al., eds, *Anschlüsse: Versuche nach Michel Foucault*. Tübingen: Edition Diskord, pp. 141–6.

Kittler, F. 1987. Nachwort. In A. M. Turing, *Intelligence Service: Schriften*. Berlin: Brinkmann und Bose, pp. 211–33.

Kittler, F., 1990. *Discourse Networks 1800/1900*. Trans. M. Metteer and C. Cullens. Intro. D. Wellbery. Stanford, CA: Stanford University Press.

Kittler, F., 1991. *Dichter Mutter Kind*. Munich: Fink.

Kittler, F., 1993a. Synergie von Mensch und Maschine. In F. Rötzer and S. Rogenhofer, eds, *Kunst machen? Gespräche über die Produktion von Bildern*. Munich: Boer, pp. 83–102.

Kittler, F., 1993b. Geschichte der Kommunikationsmedien. In J. Huber at al., eds, *Raum und Verfahren*. Basel and Frankfurt: Stroemfeld/Roter Stern, pp. 169–88.

Kittler, F., 1994. World-Breath. On Wagner's Media Technology. In D. Levine, ed., *Opera through Other Eyes*. Stanford, CA: Stanford California Press, pp. 215–35.

Kittler, F., 1997. *Literature Media Information Systems*. Ed. John Johnston. Amsterdam: OAP.

Kittler, F., 1998a. On the Take-Off of Operators. In T. Lenoir, ed., *Inscribing Science: Scientific Texts and the Materiality of Communication*. Stanford, CA: Stanford University Press, pp. 70–7.

Kittler, F., 1998b. Gleichschaltungen: Über Normen

und Standards der elektronischen Kommunikation. In M. Faßler and W. Halbach, eds, *Geschichte der Medien*. Munich: UTB, pp. 255–67.

Kittler, F., 1999. *Gramophone, Film, Typewriter*. Trans. and intro. G. Winthrop-Young and M. Wutz. Stanford, CA: Stanford University Press.

Kittler, F., 2000. *Eine Kulturgeschichte der Kulturwissenschaften*. Munich: Fink.

Kittler, F., 2003a. *Short Cuts*. Frankfurt: Zweitausendseins.

Kittler, F., 2003b. Pynchon und die Elektromystik. In B. Siegert and M. Krajewski, eds, *Thomas Pynchon: Archive – Geschichte – Verschwörung*. Weimar: VdG, pp. 123–36.

Kittler, F., 2003c. Heidegger und die Medien- und Technikgeschichte. In D. Thomä, ed., *Heidegger Handbuch. Leben – Werk – Wirkung*. Stuttgart: Metzler, pp. 500–4.

Kittler, F., 2004. *Unsterbliche: Nachrufe, Erinnerungen, Gespräche*. Munich: Fink.

Kittler, F., 2005. *Musen, Nymphen und Sirenen* (audio CD): Supposé.

Kittler, F., 2006a. *Musik und Mathematik I. Hellas 1: Aphrodite*. Munich: Fink.

Kittler, F., 2006b. Number and Numeral. *Theory, Culture & Society* 23(7–8): 51–61.

Kittler, F., 2006c. Thinking Colours and/or Machines. *Theory, Culture & Society* 23(7–8): 39–50.

Kittler, F., 2009. Towards an Ontology of Media. *Theory, Culture & Society* 26(2–3): pp. 23–31.

Kittler, F., 2010. *Optical Media: Berlin Lectures 1999*. Trans. A. Enns. Cambridge: Polity.

Kittler, F., and S. Banz, 1996. *Platz der Luftbrücke: Ein Gespräch*. Berlin: Oktagon.

Kittler, F., and R. Maresch, 1994. Wenn die Freiheit wirklich existiert, dann soll sie doch ausbrechen. In R. Maresch, ed., *Am Ende vorbei*. Vienna: Turia & Kant, pp. 95–129.

Kittler, F., and C. Vismann, 2001. *Vom Griechenland*. Berlin: Merve.

Kittler, F., and C. Weinberger, 2009. Das kalte Modell von Struktur. *Zeitschrift für Medienwissenschaft* 1, pp. 93–102.

Krämer, S., 2006. The Cultural Techniques of Time Axis Manipulation: On Friedrich Kittler's Conception of Media. *Theory, Culture & Society* 23(7–8): 93–109.

Kloock, D., and A. Spahr, 1997. *Medientheorien: Eine Einführung*. Munich: Fink.

Kroker, A., 1984. *Innis/McLuhan/Grant: Technology and the Canadian Mind*. Montreal: New World Perspectives.

Lotringer, S., and S. Cohen, eds, 2001. *French Theory in America*. New York: Routledge.

McLuhan, M., 1964. *Understanding Media: The Extensions of Man*. New York: McGraw-Hill.

Marx, K., and F. Engels, 1975. *Selected Correspondence*. Moscow: Progress Publishers.

Nietzsche, F., 2002. *The Antichrist and Fragments of a Shattering Mind*. Creation Books (available at: <www.creationbooks.com>).

Olson, D., 1994. *The World on Paper: The Conceptual and Cognitive Implications of Writing and Reading*. Cambridge: Cambridge University Press.

Peters, J. D., 1999. *Speaking into the Air: A History of the Idea of Communication*. Chicago, IL: University of Chicago Press.

Peters, J. D., 2008. Strange Sympathies: Horizons of German and American Media Theory. In F. Kelleter and D. Stein, eds, *American Studies as Media Studies*. Heidelberg: Winter, pp. 3–23.

Peters, J. D., 2010. Introduction: Friedrich Kittler's Light Shows. In F. Kittler (2010), pp. 1–17.

Philostratus, 2005. *Life of Apollonius of Tyana*. Ed. and trans. C. P. Jones. Cambridge, MA: Harvard University Press.

Powell. B., 1991. *Homer and the Origin of the Greek Alphabet.* Cambridge: Cambridge University Press.

Powell, L. 2008. Musik und Mathematik. Friedrich Kittlers gegenkulturelles Griechenland. *Musik und Ästhetik* 48: 94–100.

Pucci, P., 1998. *The Song of the Sirens: Essays on Homer.* Lanham, MD: Rowman & Littlefield.

Pynchon, T., 1987. *Gravity's Rainbow.* New York: Viking.

de Saussure, F., 1960. *Course in General Linguistics.* Ed. C. Bally and A. Sechehaye. London: Peter Owen.

Siegert, B., 1999. *Relays: Literature as an Epoch of the Postal System.* Trans. K. Repp. Stanford, CA: Stanford University Press.

Sophocles, 1984. *The Three Theban Plays: Antigone, Oedipus the King, Oedipus at Colonus.* Trans. R. Fagles. Harmondsworth: Penguin.

Staiger, E., 1991. *Basic Concepts of Poetics.* University Park, PA: Pennsylvania State University Press.

Stoker, B., 1975. *The Annotated Dracula.* Ed. L. Wolf. New York: Ballantine.

Taylor, P. A., and J. L. Harris, 2005. *Digital Matters: Theory and Culture of the Matrix.* London and New York: Routledge.

Vismann, C., 2008. *Files: Law and Media Technology.* Trans. G. Winthrop-Young. Stanford, CA: Stanford University Press.

Wade-Gery, H, T., 1952. *The Poet of the Iliad.* Cambridge: Cambridge University Press.

Wellbery, D., 1990. Foreword. In F. Kittler (1990), pp. vii–xxxiii.

Whitehead, A. N., 1978. *Process and Reality: An Essay in Cosmology.* New York: Free Press.

Winthrop-Young, G., 1994. Undead Networks: Information Processing and Media Boundary Conflicts in *Dracula.*

In D. Bruce and A. Purdy, eds, *Literature and Science*. Amsterdam and Atlanta, GA: Rodopi, pp. 107–29.

Winthrop-Young, G. 2000. Silicon Sociology, or, Two Kings on Hegel's Throne? Kittler, Luhmann and the Posthuman Merger of German Media Theory. *Yale Journal of Criticism* 13(2): 391–420.

Winthrop-Young, G. 2002. Drill and Distraction in the Yellow Submarine: The Dominance of War in Friedrich Kittler's Media Theory. *Critical Inquiry* 28(4): 825–54.

Winthrop-Young, G., 2005. *Friedrich Kittler zur Einführung*. Hamburg: Junius.

Winthrop-Young, G., 2006a. Cultural Studies and German Media Theory. In G. Hall and C. Birchall, eds, *New Cultural Studies: Adventures in Theory*. Edinburgh: Edinburgh University Press, pp. 88–104.

Winthrop-Young, G. 2006b. Implosion and Intoxication: Kittler, a German Classic, and Pink Floyd. *Theory, Culture & Society* 23(7–8): 75–91.

Winthrop-Young, G., 2008. Von gelobten und verfluchten Medienländern: Kanadischer Gesprächsvorschlag zu einem deutschen Theoriephänomen. *Zeitschrift für Kulturwissenschaften* 2: 113–28.

Winthrop-Young, G., and N. Gane. 2006. Friedrich Kittler: An Introduction. *Theory, Culture & Society* 23(7–8): 5–16.

Winthrop-Young, G., and M. Wutz, 1999. Friedrich Kittler and German Media Discourse Analysis. In Kittler (1999), pp. xi–xxxvii.

Wutz, M., 2009. *Enduring Words: Literary Narrative in a Changing Media Ecology*. Tuscaloosa, AL: University of Alabama Press.

Zuse, K., 1993. *The Computer – My Life*. Berlin: Springer.

INDEX